CORN, CROWN,
and
CONFLAGRATION

*A Memoir of an Invasion on Indigenous Soil and a
Reminder that One Reaps What One Sows*

J.A.M. Kinsella

Fulton Books
Meadville, PA

Published by Fulton Books 2022

Book Cover was designed by Travis Tubinaghtewa

ISBN 978-1-63860-769-4 (paperback)
ISBN 978-1-63860-770-0 (digital)

Printed in the United States of America

*To all who have died at the hands of regimes
from times past and the present time. Regimes
which may be here, there, or anywhere.*

DISCLAIMER

This book has been written with the best intentions and to the best of my knowledge regarding the Navajo and Hopi people. However, I am not an anthropologist or member of either tribe. Therefore, I have limited experience and knowledge regarding the cultural practices of the Navajo and Hopi. In fact, some of their ceremonies are too sacred to be written down. To respect the sanctity of tribal ceremonies, I have written about ceremonies that are not actually practiced. Rather, they are inspired by the research I could find regarding the true ceremonies which are in this book solely for an interesting plot.

This book has been written with the intention of exposing the injustices forced onto Native American people. So please eagerly learn the message in this book but respect the beliefs of the people this book is about.

Guiding thoughts:

1. *If Nazi Germany came to the realization that what they were doing was wrong, closed all concentration camps, and stopped killing Jews, would they suddenly become a good country?*
2. *If Nazi Germany gave reparations to those they tried to annihilate, would that be enough to appease the damage they did to the millions of people they killed?*
3. *Are reparations enough to erase the legacy of the Holocaust?*

A LETTER FROM THE AUTHOR

The People Who Never Smiled

Dear Reader,

Thank you for choosing to read my book. As the author, I hope to provide you with novel knowledge while entertaining your imagination. Before you embark upon the adventures in this book, please allow me to introduce myself. I am J. A. M. Kinsella, an atypical person who lives in a dictatorship. While I am mostly an autism rights advocate, my aim is to facilitate a world where all people can thrive regardless of ability. The most direct interpretation of my advocacy focuses on people with disabilities living in a world built against them. But my idea of ability extends beyond us. In it, I include the "disabling" oppression racial minorities face whenever they try to thrive.

While I have not experienced the discrimination that racial minorities endure firsthand, the exclusion and contempt I receive for having autism enable me to empathize with others. That is why I am writing a book about Native Americans despite not being a racial minority.

That said, when I began this adventure, I felt out of place. Names like J. A. M. Kinsella are rarely associated with Native Americans. In truth, the history and rights of Native Americans are a far reach from my "typical" advocacy. However, my atypical self-interests and desires to help people diverge from what most people consider "normal" anyways. For instance, my desire to help Native Americans stems from a weekend, long ago.

I call the country I live in the Regime due to its massive size and voracious appetite for consuming smaller hegemonies. To keep tabs on all citizens, the Regime is divided into sub-regimes called states. My home state includes a place called the Peninsula, which is full of beautiful evergreen trees and breathtakingly blue water. On the Peninsula, there are many designated spaces for the Aboriginal people of the land called Native American reservations. So it only makes sense that it was on the Peninsula where I encountered Native Americans in a way that altered my opinion about the Regime.

Many years ago, my family decided to enjoy a long weekend on the Peninsula. Before arriving at our rented cabin, we made a trip to a nearby grocery store. We shopped in an economically deprived town full of downtrodden residents.

While most residents lived in poverty, Native Americans were the most depressed. It was while shopping that I saw the sad state of Native Americans for the first time in my life. As my family was waiting in line to purchase groceries for the long weekend, my attention was drawn to two downtrodden people who would forever change my perspective on my life and the country I live in.

I noticed two Native American men in line to purchase their groceries the next isle over. These men wore clothes that were so threadbare, they resembled loose rags sewn together. One of the two men was morbidly obese and appeared to be in poor health. This man sat in a motorized wheelchair, an expense I question how the family could afford based on his destitute appearance. Both men pulled back their long dark hair which appeared to be prematurely turning gray. But of all the sad aspects of the observed people's appearances, their faces caught my attention the most. Dark half-moons loomed under the men's red eyes as if many nights were spent awake mourning their fate and what has been stolen from them. Their lips were firmly downturned as if frozen in that position from perpetual despair. This made them appear to frown permanently so that neither man looked as if he had ever smiled or laughed in his whole life.

After paying for groceries, my family went to the cabin. But regardless of what book I read or what interesting creatures I saw inhabiting the tide pools, the image of the disparaged Native Americans lurked in my mind. I still remember these people even though I haven't seen either of them again. But those two men whose names I don't even know inspired this book.

One day, a class I was taking assigned me to read about the Navajo and Hopi tribes. What I read intrigued me, so I extended my research beyond the confines of the classroom. To pursue my growing interest in the Navajo and Hopi people, I began reading history and anthropology books about those cultures.

While I was researching their histories, I discovered the oppression and genocide they suffered at the hands of my own country. While I have yet to conclude my research, what I have learned has enabled me to understand the gloomy appearance of the Native Americans I saw in that grocery store many years ago.

I now know that the privileges I have as a citizen of the Regime stem directly from the dirty deeds of my ancestors. While I have no control over my predecessor's choices, I do have control over my actions of remedying their malevolence.

On a final note, my prompting to do the right thing is inspired by the words of another person with autism: "This world will not be destroyed by those who do evil but by those who watch others do evil without stopping them" (Albert Einstein).

As a nonindigenous person, I have the privilege to ignore what my ancestors did to Native Americans and still reap all the benefits of their destruction. Today, I chose to do the right thing regardless of the empire I am in.

I hope you enjoy the book!

With the hope of creating a world where all people can thrive regardless of ability,

J. A. M. Kinsella

PROLOGUE

As a child, I was fortunate to have a roof over my head and loving and attentive parents. The fun, carefree days of my youth are a time the responsibility burdened grownup I have become longs for. But of all happy childhood memories, one seems particularly pertinent to this story. Under the hot sun of early July, my mother pulled a wagon I rode in for a parade. Fit for the occasion, the wagon was decorated by flags and balloons. My face was painted red, white, and blue to match my outfit. Likewise, the surrounding wagons, children in them, and their parents were also donning inane patriotic attire. I really enjoyed being a part of this Fourth of July parade, especially since I had a big bag of candy in front of me. Apparently, I was supposed to throw the candies at the onlookers we passed. Instead, I acted like the country whose birthday we were celebrating by eating the bulk of what was I was supposed to share with others. Candy aside, the patriotism I was exposed to that day gave me a sense of belonging and purpose to something larger than myself. Afterall, what's not to like about a country filled with seemingly endless "amber waves of grain" and buildings so tall that they appeared to part the sky. The citizens of this country were hardworking, entrepreneurial, and optimistic. These character traits were reflected everywhere, giving a false impression that all was well. In truth, this country had a very grim history with a secret so horrible that the government did everything within its power to keep its taxpayers from knowing about it. Yet despite all governmental attempts at censoring truth, facts prevailed.

The country in question—along with all its opulence, sky-scrapers, and amber waves of grain—exists no more.

Instead, a great fire incinerated this grand empire with red and yellow flames gorging on a buffet of infrastructure. Furious flames forced the towering buildings to fall from the sky. Freshly paved roads were liquefied as the fire spread across the land resembling molten rivers in hell. The voracious fire gorged itself for days on end until the selfish government was scorched to the earth. Now all that remains is a scene where hell appears to be extinguished and ash falls in place of snow. As a child who enjoyed the spoils of this land, I never thought I would grow up to write about this country's demise. Back then, I didn't know that I was living in a dictatorship. But even now, it feels foreign and unnatural to juxtapose my younger self wolfing down candy during a Fourth of July parade to the person I have become, a grownup who gladly writes about my country's extinction. How this happened is a story that began when three ships sailed across a sea.

*****

Three brown boats topped by white sails traveled a sapphire sea in a single file line. The mariners aboard this adventure have been sailing for months. They were convinced they were pioneering a much-needed trade route for which their names will be immortalized. Unbeknown to them, the trade route they are pursuing doesn't exist.

Their only discovery after months of exploring is that they inhabit a vast world of nothing but the ocean. But that is about to change. Out of the endless blueness, their fate changes when "Land ho!" is bellowed from the scout in the leading ship's crow nest. Relieved to be freed from an overpowering world of blue, sailors crowd the decks of their boats and marvel over the strange sight of a sprawling coastline topped with lush verdant trees.

Hope follows the sighting of land after the lengthy sea voyage, and finding land temporarily ensures that their expedition is successful. Eager to confirm their location, the crew anchors their ships off a coast they wrongly believe to be in Asia. The crew of European men donned in big hats and heavy coats excitedly boards rowboats to explore the mysterious island ahead. Strange animals swim beneath the vessels they row. The men are awestruck by unusual creatures that have yet to be studied and described in encyclopedias.

When the shore is reached, the rowboats become surrounded by footprints of brown leather boots that etch the white sand of land that will forever be changed by this arrival. These mariners are certain that they are in Asia, but exactly where remains a mystery. No words are spoken as these men take in unexpected surroundings.

Suddenly the silence is broken when someone shouts "Indian!" while pointing at a human retreating into a thick jungle. Eager to attain knowledge of their location, sailors abandon their rowboats and chase the Indian. The rest of the day is spent with sweat beading their foreheads as the crew wanders deeper into a thick tropical forest but fail to find who they're after. The farther the crew goes, the more convinced they are that they will never see her again.

Eventually, dusky red streaks the indigo sky, prompting the men to return to their larger ships before nightfall. But when they turn around, the crew realizes they are surrounded by the inhabitants of the island.

Still believing they are in Asia, the confused men are led to a populace that had yet to be studied by ethnologists and anthropologists. A bonfire highlights the strange tattoos on the muscular bodies of the lean, short, and half-naked masses. Despite never having contact with these foreigners, the Natives of the island hospitably give the European explorers food and a place to sleep. The next morning, the Natives point the Europeans in the direction of the continent.

Conquistadors meet the indigenous Taino and Carib peoples of the Caribbean in 1492.

As the three ships approach the mainland, natives fishing in their fibrous canoes paddle over to the Europeans in greeting. Exiting their hardwood rowboats, brown leather boots now imprint the white sand of the continent's shore. Curious about these visitors, the indigenous mainlanders who were fishing moments prior decide to lead the weary sailors to the heart of the city.

On the way, square, gray structures loom above a trail that weaves through multitudes of lush green vegetation. The plant variety here are outnumbering those of any European arboretum in 1492. The newcomers are enchanted by everything they see. With a starstruck gaze and open mouth, the foreigners take in their surroundings and move slowly. Guides fear that the European men being escorted into the city would forever remain in a trance at what is before them if they are not encouraged to keep moving. After much prompting, stopping, and finally walking, the city is reached.

As the explorers entered the city, the gray squares that they saw looming over the tops of trees are massive stones forming layered pyramids. Amazingly, no mortar is seen or felt in the cracks between. Yet the boulders stack up perfectly without gaps, soaring into the sky. This accomplished construction puzzles the Europeans who know nothing but the rickety wood and crumbly brick shacks of their homeland. Back home, cities in Europe housing thousands of residents suffer frequently from disease, dysentery, and death. Unlike Native Americans, who had sewer systems, Europeans relieved themselves in chamber pots, which were commonly emptied out windows. As a result, urine wetted the city streets of Europe, and floating solid waste in towns was common.

In this new world, the foreigners enter a city with a population exceeding any the crew had ever encountered in their life. Unlike Europe, the people of this new land appear to get along amicably, and waste is nonexistent.

As they walk, smells of freshly ground, potent spices waft toward the voyagers. Bright, juicy, freshly picked fruits and the salivating scent of meat grilling over open flames captivates the voyagers. The crew also admires large sculptures, art unlike anything known. But what intrigues the Europeans most is the presence of gold. Precious and rare in the old world, gold appears to abound in this new land. All observed citizens wear gold jewelry. Gold dust gilds buildings and statues. The sun radiates off all of this gold, coating everything in a soft, ethereal warm glow like the fabled gold brick streets of heaven.

At the epicenter of the city, the weary voyagers are given a cushioned bed for the night. Much to their delight, they finally get to satisfy their cravings for the exotic fruits and smoked meats they passed while exploring the city.

In bed, the Europeans relive the events of the day and wonder if they are in Asia after all. These foreigners ought to be thankful to their indigenous hosts for welcoming them and treating them to so much hospitality. Instead, the voyagers focus solely on the profits that can be made from exploiting the resources of this new land. But beyond profits, each man secretly fears what will happen when these advanced Americans discover the backward ways of Europeans.

Conquest and monarchy have been the cornerstones of European civilization. As a result, few Europeans live to reach adulthood. Most are impoverished and die in childhood from starvation, diseases, and destitution. Unhappy as most people are about Western civilization, they accept it because they know nothing else. But a populous city, which rivals heaven and houses millions of peaceful people, challenges the most rudimentary support for Eurocentrism.

If the voyagers were peasants, perhaps they would delight over an affluent society that treats citizens more equitably than those back home. None of these sailors were born into the ruling class, but they were all born into affluent families. As such, the greed these traveling men inherited corrupts their ethics.

To ensure that only those who sailed across the ocean on this one voyage benefit from the spoils of this new land, a sailor councils Columbus, the facilitator of this journey, "I fear that these nations are capable of uprooting and destroying Europe because their society is beyond ours. To prevent the Americans from challenging our customs, upper class, and religion, we must destroy them and take everything from them, especially gold. After pilfering their land, we will ensure the preservation of our White ways." Columbus agreed with this flawed sentiment. Shortly thereafter, the grand empires of the Americas were reduced to rubble.

The pyramids of Mesoamerica are one of many building feats accomplished before 1492. These pyramids, like most ancient American buildings, are made entirely of stacked stones held together without mortar or cement. In these cities'

life was abundant and relatively peaceful. At the time of Columbus's arrival, the Mayan Empire had over eight hundred thousand residents. Despite the multitude of inhabitants, the Mayan Empire rarely struggled with the issues of sanitation and civil unrest, which were normal in European societies at the time of Columbus's voyage. Many pyramids were built in the Old World. However, civilizations of the Old World were more connected to each other and had the ability to share knowledge concerning great building feats. The American's ability to build grand fortresses like this, despite being isolated from the shared knowledge of the Old World, reveals their true genius. On a sidenote, Columbus visited the Mayan Empire on his fourth voyage to the Americas in 1523. The author has blurred this timeline and route of Columbus's ships to make the story more interesting.

The centuries following the arrival of Columbus have been filled with brutal persecution toward Native Americans. Governments occupying the indigenous soil of the American continents promote beliefs that Native Americans are stupid, backward, and unaccomplished. Europeans, on the other hand, are portrayed as benevolent bringers of civilization. In truth, Europeans slaughtered millions of indigenous people who had lived their best life before 1492.

Most governments occupying the American continents are affluent and sometimes opulent. But of all who benefit from the affluence of these governments, Native Americans benefit the least. In one country, the United States of America, Native Americans have the highest rates of suicide, alcoholism, domestic violence, and sexual abuse. Native Americans are also the most likely to live in poverty out of all ethnicities, despite only making up 1 percent of the total population.[1]

It appears that Native Americans are losing the war for existence and sovereignty in their own homeland. But it is victorious that they even exist in spite of governments that want them dead. By surviving and even thriving, Native Americans expand their influence and gain the power to turn the tables in their favor.

While all survivors of the United States of America have the power to destroy the parasitic government, the author believes that two of the remaining tribes have the greatest potential. Unfortunately, usurping European domination is complicated by the loyalties of each tribal member, for survivors have the potential to become the best ally to the United States of America or its worst enemy. One of the two tribes is written about in this book. The other tribe in this book will either be an accomplice or an antagonist to the first tribe's agenda.

THE GREATEST COUNTRY EVER

There is a land straddled between two shinning seas dominated by a fearsome empire called the Regime. Ocean boundaries surrounding Regime citizens appear infinite to those on the coastlines. For this reason, many citizens falsely believe that this country is the only one on earth. Contrarily, all oceans are finite and break upon a shore somewhere else.

Regime citizens can't see beyond the curving sapphire seas and they rarely think about the world beyond their beach. Instead, they narrow their minds to their empire's amber waves of grain which are farmed on the outskirts of gleaming cities. Each Regime city is full of buildings ascending into the sky, which house the most prosperous corporations in human history. Towering buildings are parted by expansive highways that always lead to the capitol. Wealth is abundant from the empire's successful trade and business. This influx of money creates a flawless veneer.

The empire's flawless appearance paired with a narrow worldview discourages citizens from leaving the Regime. Instead, they insist a god created beyond the sapphire seas blesses the country from the mountains to the prairies to the oceans white with foam. Blind love for this country is further egged on by the Regime's nickname, Land of the Free. Aptly named because Regime citizens enjoy more freedoms and privileges than people of any other country.

As a result, most Regime citizens are phenomenally patriotic with unwavering loyalty to their rulers; and why wouldn't they? After all, governors insist that all citizens who pay the landlord's salary through their tax dollars live in the best country ever. Who wouldn't want to live there?

Unfortunately, contradicting its flawless appearance, the Regime regularly inflicts woe upon its citizens. Yet the vast distance between the Regime and the rest of the world enables landlords to escape consequences for unethical protocols. As for citizen's freedoms, inconsistencies exist between what is promised and what is delivered.

Few people benefit from the Regime's economy. The opulent less than 1 percent of this hegemony are among the richest in the world. Fortunately, some prosperous people generously donate portions of their money to the impoverished.

Unfortunately, the bulk of ultra-wealthy citizens hoard their money. Money hoarding never bothers those in power because it results in a gleaming landscape creating the false impression that all is well. Above all else, the opulent 1 percent line the politician's pockets to keep making schemes.

Moneyed citizens wasted millions to keep the impoverished majority silent. But eventually, the silent majority got tired of being shortchanged and challenged the entire government. Despite the Regime's domineering and impenetrable appearance, citizens recently destroyed it. Even the most successful companies failed to bail it out. Today, there are no longer amber waves of grain or elaborate corporate buildings towering over the impoverished. One must read further to understand why. This book is the untimely obituary of the Regime and a story of how ordinary citizens reduced a grand empire to ashes.

Few people survived the Regime's inferno. But the survivors won't complain about the empire's death. The majority of citizens in the Land of the Free were miserable.

Most Regime citizens struggled to survive on their working wages. If one stood on a patio high rise of a corporation and looked down at the streets below, they would see the dwelling places of vagabonds, poor people who could not afford to put a roof over their heads.

Despite the mainstream poverty in this opulent land, food was abundant. Landlords combated starvation because it would tarnish their image. Their solution was to genetically modify and mass-produce amber waves of grain. Harvested grain deprived of most nutrients could be sold cheaply. This nutrient-deficient food called junk food was a staple to the Regime. Its cheapness enabled destitute citizens to fill their stomachs. Consequently, the nutrient deficits and sweetness of this high-caloric food replaced starvation with poor health and obesity.

Obesity resulted in an array of health complications that overwhelmed the Regime's healthcare system. As a result, citizens were left to suffer from treatable diseases. Most people never saw recovery and died at the hands of governing landlords who insisted they lived in the best country ever. But as nonchalant as landlords were regarding the well-being of citizens, they were even more negligent with gun control. Poorly regulated gun stores blessed the hopeless huddled masses. At least they could kill themselves by way of the bullet and be freed from living in this land.

One would think Regime citizens were well aware of their strife. However, the oceans distancing Regime citizens from other countries prevented easy comparison. Beyond this geographic isolation, the Regime landlords nurtured citizen ignorance.

Pervasive entertainment called "unreality TV" was as prevalent as poverty and junk food. It was designed by the government to distract citizens from seeing the extent of their struggles. We all have the potential to build a better world for ourselves and others. Regime landlords didn't want their captives to know this. Instead, Regime governors created zealous patriots by convincing citizens that they perpetually owed their country. This brainwashing caused citizens to refuse any suggestion that the Regime was not as good as they believed.

But racism was the epitome of Regime malevolence. The financial backbone of the Land of the Free was rooted in slave labor. Landlords abolished slavery when the Industrial Revolution replaced free human exploits with machine labor. Yet the roots of slavery created an institution of racism. People from Africa were perpetually persecuted in the Land of the Free. Over the years, little progress had been made to alleviate the trauma descendants of slavery suffer.

This unfortunate truth begs two questions ignorant citizens never pondered. How could any country built upon the backbreaking horrors of slavery call itself the Land of the Free or, worse yet, claim to be the best country ever?

Beyond the unhealed wounds of slavery existed a more sinister sin. This sin was so severe that landlords kept it under lock and key. For this sin was the secret truth of the Regime. Despite the Regime's best efforts at censoring truth, citizens eventually discovered the secret. When they did, the silent majority usurped the Regime entirely.

The most sobering truth about the Land of the Free is that it is not free at all. Landlords reigning over this parcel of earth are actually dictators who invaded Native American soil.

Millions of indigenous peoples inhabited this land long before European conquerors implemented the Regime. Therefore, the land in question is not free land. It is stolen land that belongs to the Native Americans. This truth was the Regime's Achilles heel.

Regime governors feared what would happen to their empire when citizens realized that they were on Native American tribal lands or, worse yet, the true history of their country. Unreality TV was vigorously dispatched to prevent citizens from knowing the truth and forcing people into a state of permanent hebetude. So effective was the Unreality TV that few people in the Regime ever heard the word indigenous. Ignorant citizens thought Native Americans only existed as derogatory mascots for sports teams and offensive costumes for scary holidays.

Alas, the presidents failed to realize that a day would come when every government on earth would repent to the rest of the world for their sins. Despite all attempts at defying retribution, the day of penance for the Regime came and passed. No one saw it coming. In truth, leaders of the Regime believed they had everything under control to the point that destruction seemed impossible.

Yet there was an ancient prophecy about the Regime's destruction and demise. The Hopi tribe had foretold that millions of people would suffer. If only the landlords of the Regime had listened. If only the citizens of the Regime had educated themselves and treated the first people of the land decently. Perhaps then fewer people would have perished in anguish.

THE HOPI PEOPLE

The Regime also known as the United States of America, is a dictatorship that slaughters Indigenous people. In the past few centuries, the Regime has extended its own borders by brutally robbing Native Americans of their homeland. Today, only 574 federally recognized tribes composing one percent of the Regime's total population have survived the genocide on "American" soil.

Research has yet to conclude how many people inhabited US soil before Columbus arrived. Current estimates hypothesize that five million Native Americans lived in the area now occupied by the Regime in AD 1200. Population studies assert the native population to have increased and significantly surpassed five million people by the time Columbus arrived.[1]

Today's reduced population of Native Americans continues to suffer from the engulfing empire. But a spark of hope remains. After centuries of pilfering Indigenous lands, separating families, and murdering the inhabitants, the "gracious" Regime gifted each tribe a small mercy. As compensation, Natives have been bequeathed small slivers of land "reserved" for them from within their own homeland.

Hope for cultural survival exists on reservations because they are sovereign and are run by tribal governments. Residents living with their tribe create a neighborhood full of their specific Indigenous cultures, forming a community that is hard to find elsewhere. Some tribes use their sovereignty to preserve their language by making it and American English the official languages on the reservation. But a shadow looms over the hope that these "sovereign" reservations offer.

The Regime constantly whittles away at reservation borders despite kindly returning that reserved land to the first people. Life on reservations is ungainly for residents. For they live in a sovereign nation enclaved inside an aggressive land and resource-hungry empire. Furthermore, Native Americans are required to pay income and sales taxes to the Regime despite living on sovereign parcels of land the Regime stole from and then returned to them. Adding to this unfairness is the fact that Native American microcultures are frequently endangered. Contrarily, the Regime has an influential and affluent macro-culture with a global reach.

A second small mercy is the Bureau of Indian Affairs (BIA). This organization is funded by tax dollars and is responsible for ensuring that the basic needs of Native Americans are met. However, the BIA is underfunded and overwhelmed by the needs of 574 tribes. Therefore, the BIA frequently fails to adequately help all residents of any one reservation. This outcome leaves many Native Americans feeling that the money they pay in taxes never benefits them.

The twisted history between the Regime and reservations has forced Native Americans into unique struggles few people can empathize with. But of all the challenges tribes are oppressed by, the Hopi tribe has a particularly difficult circumstance.

The Hopi are the westernmost group of the Pueblo peoples. Puebloans compose a large group of Native American tribes that branch into smaller, loose-knit societies dwelling in clay apartment abodes on cliffs. The Pueblo peoples are well known for their elaborate weavings and pottery designs. Historically, all Puebloans were peaceful, but Hopis were the epitome of peace. In fact, their name translates to "people of peace" in English.

The Hopi are agrarian like their neighbors. However, water is scarce in their high desert establishment. As such, they need thousands of acres of land to continue their lifestyle.

Unfortunately, the Regime stole two-thirds of Hopi land this past century. Instead of desecrating Hopi land as cities and farms for colonizers, the Regime gifted it to a separate Native American tribe called the Navajo.

Historically, both Hopis and Navajos have disagreed over boundaries. Until the Regime intervened, all land debates have ended peacefully with both tribes satisfied by the new verdict.

In fact, the Regime started the latest land feud in 1864 by nearly annihilating all Navajos in an internment camp. Upon return, the Navajo expanded its borders and spread its population to reduce the chance of being round up and exploited again. Worries over self-preservation prompted the Navajos to venture into the outskirts of their reservation's far north. Those who moved there infringed the Hopi Nation's property. The Hopi protested the Navajo's encroachment. In response, the Regime created a shared area for both tribes.

Hopis were satisfied with their ancestral farming plots in the shared area. The Navajo's agenda was to expand their territory. Hopis believed the Navajo encroachment violated the conditions of the shared area agreement and petitioned the Regime to send the intruders back to the Navajo Nation. Instead, the Regime ruled that the Navajo had earned unoccupied Hopi lands through settler rights. As peaceful people, the Hopi have yet to go to war against anyone. True to tradition, the Hopis peacefully moved to the three sacred mesas, the most sacred part of their land. The resulting Navajo Nation boundary now encompasses the perimeter of the Hopi Nation. The resulting imbroglio has the Hopi Nation located within the Navajo reservation all of which is enclaved inside the Regime.

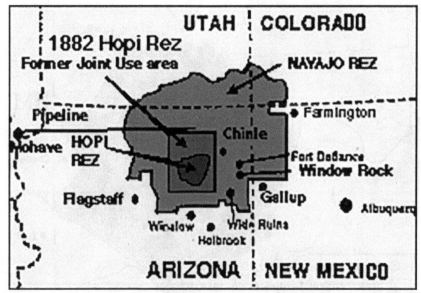

This map shows what lands the Hopi have lost to the Navajo in light red. The dotted lines running through the center of this map are the boundaries of neighboring states, and the biggest mass of red in this map is of the current Navajo Nation. The square area in the middle of the Navajo Nation was the original Hopi Nation of 1882, which later became a joint-use area between the Navajo and Hopi people but is now part of the Navajo Nation. The smallest, dark-red dot in the middle of the red square is the Hopi Nation of today.

The Regime allowed the Navajo to consume Hopi land because of the fallacious belief that all Native Americans share one culture. In truth, Hopis and Navajos are more different than similar. Religion is one of both tribes' many differences. The Hopi refer to caves on their land as shrines called Kivas, which they believe to be homes for Hopi Kachina deities. Hopis can freely communicate with Kachinas by entering a Kiva.

Unlike the Hopi, the Navajo religion lacks kivas and preaches of distant deities who can only be reached by prayer. When the Navajo annexed Hopi land, they overtook Hopi Kivas. Hopis who want to practice their religion on ancestral land must now traverse into the Navajo Nation to access their Kiva shrines. Thus far, the Navajo have not desecrated the Hopi Kivas. But having shrines of a different religion on one's land causes friction.

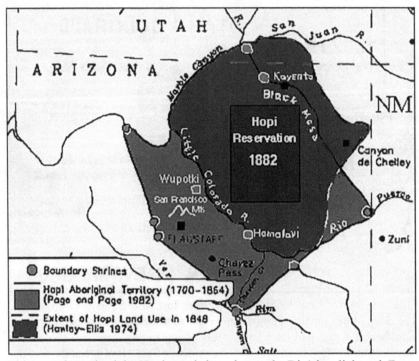

This map shows land the Hopi people have lost to the Dinè in a light red. From this map one can also see how many Hopi Kivas are in the Navajo Nation. The darker red color in the middle was a joint-use area for both Navajo and Hopi people.

Another source of friction is the vast geographic barrier the Navajo Nation created between the Hopi Nation and the rest of the world. As the largest reservation in the Regime, the immense northern region of the Navajo Nation surrounding the Hopi Nation, which is mostly bereft of paved roads, electricity, and running water. Worst yet, the Hopi endure additional challenges the Navajo are spared from. For instance, the Navajo have adapted well to change and have attained broad global recognition that aids their cultural preservation. This recognition the Navajo have received helps them acquire aid in times of need.

On the other hand, the Hopi are a small tribe with only 18,327 members and have received little recognition over the years. As a consequence, the plight of the Hopi is frequently overlooked.

Most people know challenges such as the Hopi-Navajo land dispute from the Navajo perspective only. Being distanced and overlooked has also resulted in a phenomenally high unemployment rate of the Hopi Nation. So despite living in an opulent country to which they must pay taxes, the Hopi experience third-world challenges worsened by isolation.

Resiliently, the Hopi have fiercely clung to their culture. They even manage to live productive, happy lives in the face of these seemingly insurmountable obstacles. Religion continues to be the Hopi's greatest inspiration for finding joy amid hardship.

The Hopi believe that they are the caretakers of earth. As such, they feel responsible for protecting the well-being of all who reside here. They fulfill this duty through dances and prayers to heal anyone in need. Committed to being people of peace, the Hopi bless and pray for those who have hurt them. The Hopi extend kindness where they have not received it because they believe that malice is wrong, and the most natural state of existence is love.

Hopi religion also asserts that the Hopi are experienced peoples with an ancient lineage. Their lore claims their ancestors have lived in three previous worlds, each containing a grand challenge to surmount and remember.

Learning from the challenges of the first three worlds encourages the Hopi to believe in eventual success regardless of circumstances. Above all else, the Hopi find solace in believing that they are not eternal inhabitants of earth. Eventually, the Kachina deities will rescue them from this fourth world and send them to a fifth world. Until then, the Hopi are dedicated to nurturing their current world.

According to their lore, the Hopi entered this current fourth world as freshly planted seeds. After germinating in spirit, the ground opened, and the sun welcomed the Hopis by extending an outpouring of light. They followed the sun's instructions and stood up straight on the surface of the earth. The sun then told the Hopi to find the center of the universe. After walking miles and leaving a spiral trail, the Hopi reached the third of the three sacred mesas. Stars then aligned, signifying arrival at the center of the universe.

The alignment of stars above was accompanied by an abundance of flowers below. The petals created a rainbow of color extending as far as the eye could see below. After witnessing this beauty, the sun instructed the Hopi to bloom on the mesas like the carpeting flowers. The sun then retreated into the sky, leaving the Hopi on the mesas. Against all odds, the Hopi have remained on the mesas despite the ardent desires and efforts of other people to remove them.

The Hopi creation story might sound illogical to those who haven't been exposed to such beliefs before. However, Hopi beliefs collide with science in a unique way. Scientists hypothesize that the first people to enter the American continents did so through the Bering Strait. Large ice sheets blocked out most of the North American continent when the Hopi's ancestors first accessed the Americas. As such, their only option was to settle in an area now called the Regime's southwest. Science doesn't specifically name the first peoples of the Americas. But it does align with the Hopi's claim that all Native Americans descended from people who settled in the Regime's southwest territory.

Furthermore, the Hopi village of Oraibi on the third mesa is the oldest, continuously occupied area of the American continents. Globally, Hopi culture is among the most ancient cultures still in existence today. Their ancient and unique culture captivates the anthropologists who also advocate for their cultural protection.

Yet a more interesting avenue of cultural survival has to do with the Navajo. Both Hopi and Navajo are ancient neighbors with many encounters and exchanges of ideas. Some Hopi beliefs have been acculturated into Navajo traditions. Their more popularized culture and broader global influence give the Navajo greater leverage in sharing acculturated Hopi traditions with the world, thereby passively preserving them.

Kachina dolls are the most common Hopi rite practiced by the Navajo. Kachina dolls are carvings of Kachina deities or other sacred entities. They are carved from the root of a cottonwood tree by spiritual men. Cottonwood is used to symbolize birth and the tree's root is used to symbolize grounding. Kachina dolls are elaborately carved, with hands and feet in reciprocated positions. Extensive attention to detail is used for painting Kachinas because painting is the only decoration Hopis employ.

The Navajo whose religion lacks Kachina deities make Kachina dolls to symbolize sacred objects. Navajo Kachinas wear fur or jewelry, and their Kachinas typically lack hands and feet. Hopi Kachinas are strictly made from cottonwood roots, but Navajo Kachinas are made from many types of wood. Both tribal nations handle Kachina dolls with the utmost respect. However, unlike the Navajo, the Hopi believe that everything is alive and soulful. To the Hopi, a carved Kachina doll is literally the deity it represents—holiness enshrined in wood. Having Kachina dolls at home guarantees to the Hopi that the gods are physically among people.[10]

Kachina deities are also believed to be corporal and close. For six months of the year, Kachinas dwell in the San Francisco mountains of New Mexico. After the winter solstice, Kachinas travel to the mesas. They arrive in the heat of summer when prayers for rain are most fervent. It is during this hot and dry time of year that the holiest of Hopi rites, the Snake Dance, is performed for the visiting Kachina deities.

The Snake Dance takes two weeks of preparation under scorching desert sun. Snakes are collected and the Snake Dancers become spiritually pure through meditation and fasting. Snakes are danced with because the Hopi believe that snakes are direct messengers to the gods. Dancing with snakes ensures that the Hopi's prayers for rain are heard. The Kachinas not only watch the Snake Dance for entertainment but also judge how kind the people are. If the Kachinas observe that the Hopi are faithful in executing the snake dance, and demonstrate good character, prayers for rain will be answered. As long as the Hopi remember the Kachinas, the Kachinas will remember and protect the Hopi.[11]

Some of the many Hopi Kachina dolls.

Kachina deities have given the Hopi a string of nine prophecies to track their time in this current fourth world. A sign is attached to each prophecy, so an observant Hopi will know when each one has been fulfilled. Eight of the nine prophecies have already been fulfilled.

The first prophecy warns of a collision between people: "There will be a coming of white-skinned men who strike their enemies with thunder." This prophecy was fulfilled in 1492 when Columbus and a crew of white-skinned Europeans landed in the Caribbean. Guns were the crew's weapon of choice, and they boomed like thunder with every shot fired. Many Europeans followed Columbus's route to the Americas, armed with their own thundering guns.

The other half of the first prophecy serves as a warning: "The white-skinned men will destroy the earth and many temptations will follow, distracting people from truth." Hopis are instructed to stay true to their religion and culture despite the temptations offered by White people. The Hopi are also instructed not to hate Europeans despite the fact that most Europeans have treated them brutally. For Hopi religion teaches that all people are of one extended family. Therefore, it is the *actions* of Europeans that are evil, not the *essence* of everyone from Europe. So the true fight for continuation is not a war between indigenous and Europeans, rather a fight between good and evil. The only way to win is through peace.

The second prophecy predicted that "there will be a spinning of wheels with many voices." After the Regime was established, many Europeans ventured west in prairie wagons. Perhaps the "spinning of wheels" was fulfilled by the spinning wheels of the prairie wagons venturing west. As more wheels spun west, the presence of Europeans increased. Bustling cities were built, and a once-quiet landscape was polluted not just by many voices but also by the foreigners' vehicles and electronic devices.

The third prophecy predicted the emergence of a new animal: "There will come a strange beast, like a buffalo with long horns." An iconic animal fitting this picture is the Texas longhorn. It descended from the first cows brought to Hispaniola by Columbus in 1493. Spaniards expanded their invasion from the Caribbean to the American southwest with their imported cows. Cows escaped the conquistador's ranches marked by a subsequent multitude of feral cow hoof prints altering the pure earth. Feral cattle grew in population, developing long horns, resilience, and strength. When pioneers ventured west, the hardy traits of longhorns and the fact that feral cows were free, made them a prized choice of livestock for the penniless pioneers. Eventually, all feral longhorns were returned to ranches, and they developed a widespread presence across the Regime.[13]

The fourth prophecy predicts a metallic alteration to the land: "The land will be crossed with snakes of metal." As the Regime expanded, the need for connecting the east and west coasts became necessary. Steel was forged, and an efficient network of rails was laid to connect citizens across the Regime. These railroad tracks still "snake" their way throughout the land the Regime occupies. Perhaps as a fulfillment of the fourth prophecy.

The fifth prophecy predicted an alteration from above: "The land will be crisscrossed from above with a giant spider web." Almost everyone today uses the internet. To access the internet, people enter the world wide *web*. Interestingly, the word web is frequently used to refer to the entire internet. The normalization of the word web for a large network that connects the billions of people in this world could signalize the giant spider web prophesized. In another way, the airplanes which traverse the globe from above must follow a specific path. When all air travel routes from around the globe are combined, the result is a web-like pattern of traveling jets.

The sixth prophecy predicts a "land crisscrossed with rivers of stone that make pictures in the sun." Bulky satellites that circumnavigate earth could be compared to stones due to their heaviness and round shape. Satellites orbit the earth like a running river and use the light from the sun to take pictures. As such, one could claim that the sixth prophecy has been fulfilled by the launching of satellites.

The seventh prophecy warns people of the consequences of land desecration: "The sea will turn black, and many things will die because of it." Oil spills create black slicks of the ocean. Unfortunately, multitudes of wildlife die in the aftermath of an oil spill, providing context for the seventh prophecy's ongoing fulfillment.

The eighth prophecy predicted a time when "Long-haired youths join tribal nations to learn their ways." During the 1960s, long hair was popular in the hippie subculture. Some hippies ventured into tribal lands to gain indigenous intelligence. Many natives adopt people into their tribe so long as those who wish to join are well-behaved. The Hopi declare that anyone who is kind, well-mannered, does the right thing without compensation, and is eager to attain knowledge is a true Hopi. As such, many hippies joined the Hopi and other tribes in the 1960s.

The ninth and, so far, unfulfilled prophecy, predicts, "Dwelling places in the heavens will fall with a great crash, appearing as a blue star." The blue star mentioned in this prophecy is no ordinary star. It is the Blue Kachina deity radiating like a star. This shining broadcast warns the people of the earth that they are living the final days of this fourth world. After shining, the Blue Kachina will travel to earth, purifying it along the way.

When the Blue Kachina reaches earth, the Red Kachina deity is prophesied to shine like a star. After its bright broadcast, the Red Kachina will follow the Blue Kachina's route to earth. Upon arrival, it will destroy everything evil. In doing so, all greedy and corrupt people will be punished for their avarice. But those who are pure in heart will be spared from suffering and sent to the fifth world with the Hopis.

The Hopi decree that until the end arrives, people should live as peacefully and well-mannered as possible.[12] Despite being vague about when the world will end, most prophecies have been fulfilled. Observant Hopis suspect that the Blue and Red Kachinas will come soon. As such, it behooves everyone to heed this warning to be kind to all.

THE NAVAJO PEOPLE

Now let us explore the vast, red-sanded high desert mixed with pine forests and towering mountains composing the Navajo Nation. In the Regime, the Navajo people have the largest reservation, spanning over 27,413 square miles, which surrounds the Hopi Nation enclave, and the second-largest tribal population exceeding 399,494 people.[1] The Navajo are fortunate to have a large reservation and tribe. But the US dictatorship persecutes them in other ways.

To begin, the name "Navajo" is a misnomer. Navajos call themselves Dinè (Dinn-EH), meaning "the people." Neighboring Anasazi's called the Dinè "NA-BAY-HO," meaning "spiral corn people." This nickname reflects the Dinè belief that spirals are sacred patterns to be replicated in planting corn, melons, squash, cotton, and beans.

Spirals are sacred because the Dinè believe that people have spiral-shaped souls, which enter the body at birth during crowning. In doing so, one's spirit leaves a spiral pattern of hair follicles on their scalp. After birth, the unique spiral of a person's soul is visibly represented in their fingerprints, the palms of hands, and the soles of feet. Intriguingly, people who are not Dinè often use fingers, hands, and footprints to identify individuals on a regular basis. During death, which the Dinè call crossing over, one's soul is said to leave their bodies and manifest in a spiral apparition called Chindi. As Chindi, people are free to linger over their graves, unite with their ancestors, or be reincarnated into another life.

During the Spanish invasion, the sanctity Dinè place on spirals resulted in a name change. When the Spanish attempted to find and quell their strongest resistance, the foreign invaders asked of neighboring tribes, "Who keeps stealing and breaking our supplies?" The response was, "The Na-BAY-Ho are doing it because they want you to go home!" The nickname NA-BAY-Ho was written as *Navajo* by Spaniards. Today, most people are familiar with the name Navajo, but few know that the Navajo actually refer to themselves as Dinè.

Since the dawn of European invasions, the Dinè have repeatedly been robbed of and displaced from their ancestral land. In a tragedy called the Navajo Long Walk, the entire Dinè population was nearly annihilated. Back then, the Regime Army (US Army) ousted the Dinè from their ancestral land and callously forced them to walk over three hundred miles to an internment camp called Bosque Redondo.[13]

During two months of nonstop walking, 20 percent of the total Dinè population died from inadequate food, water, and sleep. The US Army spared itself from the same mortality fate by working in shifts, stocking, and receiving adequate provisions, and changing staff at pre-determined checkpoints. Unlike the well-prepared and fortified US Army, the Dinè were quickly rounded up and forced to march before packing for the arduous journey. As bad as the Navajo Long Walk was, the worst was yet to come.

At the camp, detainees frequently suffered disease and dysentery because Bosque Redondo lacked facilities for sanitary toileting, bathing, eating, and sleeping. This severe squalor caused another 25 percent of the remaining Dinè to die a miserable death by defilement.

All internees suffered tremendously. But those who remained steadfast to tradition were the most persecuted. Dinè people who spoke their native tongue or who practiced their traditional religion were brutally beaten and forced to cope with untreated open wounds in feculent filth. Meanwhile, Dinè who shunned their heritage, spoke English, and wore European clothes were rewarded with food, water, and a cleaner living area.

The US Army enabled the Regime to profit from Bosque Redondo's exploits. Many Native Americans who survived ethnic cleansing were sold into slavery in their own homeland. The living conditions in Bosque Redondo were so horrific that some Dinè parents actually offered to sell their own children into slavery. In a humiliating parents' "protective choice," they believed their children had a better chance at surviving as a slave than as prisoners of Bosque Redondo.

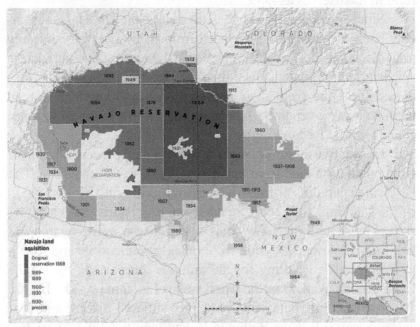

A map showing the successful Dinè land reclamation and how far away Bosque Redondo is from Dinètah, all traditional Navajo land. Thus far, land reclamation has been successful, but the Dinè have yet to take back the entirety of their land, which lies between Tsoodzil, Tsisnaasjini', Dibe Nitsaa, and Doko'o'osliid.

Four hundred miles away from Bosque Redondo, the Regime was pilfering resources from ancient Dinè land. After four years of constant theft, the Regime decided to "graciously" free the remaining Dinè internees. Before liberation, the Dinè were forced to sign a treaty with the Regime despite the fact that few Dinè understood English and could only sign the treaty with an "X."

This was the Treaty of 1868, which established the relationship between the Dinè and the Regime. Although this treaty is still in effect today, the Regime has done little to fulfill promises made long ago.

Article 13 of the treaty set aside permanent land for the Dinè, creating the Navajo Nation. Like most tribes in the Regime, the Dinè mark their land with natural boundaries. Dinè land, Dinètah, is a valley between the four sacred mountains: Tsisnaasjini' (Mount Blanca), Tsoodzil (Mount Taylor), Doko'o'osliid (the San Francisco Peaks of Arizona), and Dibè Nitsaa (Mount Hephaestus).[8] Initially, the Navajo Nation was reduced to only 10 percent of Dinè ancestral land. Since 1868, the Dinè people have been fighting for its entirety. While the Dinè have done marvelously at expanding their borders, the entirety of ancestral land has yet to be reclaimed.

This is the Navajo Nation flag. The dark square in the middle is the original reservation of 1886. The other sections symbolize successful land reclamations. The surrounding four mountains on the flag symbolize the four sacred mountains showing people the Navajo Nation's pre-Regime boundaries.

Most articles in the Treaty of 1868 could greatly benefit the Dinè, such as providing them sufficient food and water for their trek home. The Regime's Article 11 failed to communicate that they reduced Dinè land by 90 percent. But few diaspora people ever returned home. At least the Dinè who survived Bosque Redondo did.

Article 9 also benefited the survivors. As promised, livestock was given to each male head of the house who wanted to farm. While the Regime was kind enough to donate livestock, this generosity conflicted with Dinè gender roles. Traditionally, women are responsible for satisfying their families' material needs. Farming is therefore considered a female job because most Dinè families get everything they need from farming. As such, Dinè women owned all physical property because they were responsible for managing it. Giving males property conflicted with the Dinè culture of female ownership.

Of the few fulfilled articles, the final one had repercussions beyond gender confusion. Article 6 states the need to "ensure the civilization of the Indians...[making education necessary]." The Regime fulfilled this promise by building boarding schools on Dinè land. Children were forcibly removed from their families to attend school full time.

School curriculums centered around ethnic cleansing with mottos to "kill the Indian, save the man." In an attempt to "save the man," Dinè students were forbidden from and harshly punished for speaking their native tongue, wearing traditional clothes, or practicing Dinè arts. Abuse ran rampant in the boarding schools, and parents were disallowed from protecting their own children.

The few fulfilled treaty articles were not administered well. Ironically, the most beneficial articles have yet to be executed. For instance, article 8 promises that each year on September 1, the Regime would provide clothing and other basic necessities to the Dinè. Many Navajo residents live in poverty and would benefit from the fulfillment of article 8. Unfortunately, this promise is rarely fulfilled leaving the impoverished Dinè to make do with what they have.

Article 3 of the treaty promises to provide easy access to water. The Regime has completely failed to fulfill this promise. Currently 30 percent of all homes in the large Navajo Nation lack running water. Water security has always been paramount to the desert-dwelling Dinè's survival. Recently, water has become even harder to attain. The Regime's coal mining industries have polluted traditional springs forcing Dinè people to travel miles for clean water. European farming practices, which are not suited to arid climates, have been widely "encouraged" by the ruling landlords and have resulted in tighter restrictions. By failing to provide the promised water, the Regime threatens the Dinè's imperiled existence and culture.

In the Treaty of 1868, the Dinè agreed not to kill any Regime citizens, steal from passing trains, or start wars against the Regime. Historically, the Dinè have upheld their end of the bargain, but the Regime has yet to do theirs. The historical trauma the Dinè endured through ethnic cleansing and broken promises has challenged Dinè resiliency. Yet the Dinè refuse to allow oppression to consume them. Dinè ethics emphasize accountability and responsibility. They are encouraged to create the life they desire despite their adversaries. Dinè religion instructs not to say anything bad about any event, person, or consequence.

Instead of focusing on what is wrong, the Dinè strive to find peace, joy, happiness, and confidence in all aspects of life. People who manage to coexist with their surroundings are said to be in a state of Hozho or harmony. To reach Hozho, forgiveness is essential. Grudges are believed to be damaging to one's health, making the grudge holder feel dis-ease. Despite the horrors the Regime has thrust upon the Dinè, they resist malice in their interactions with the Regime and even forgive the Regime for past wrongs. The goal of coexisting with all surroundings is reflected by the most common Dinè prayer, the Beauty Way Prayer:

I will be happy forever.
Nothing will hinder me.
I walk with beauty before me. I walk with beauty behind
me. I walk with beauty above me. I walk with beauty
below me. I walk with beauty always around me.
And my words will always be beautiful.

Lines of this prayer are recited each morning to greet the new day and are repeated as needed. Each Dinè also carries a pouch of yellow corn pollen which signifies birth and connection to the Holy People. Carrying it reminds the Dinè not to overlook anything because beauty is everywhere. Each morning, pouches of yellow corn pollen are refilled, and some of it is dispersed at dawn to sanctify the day.

Proactively searching for positivity amid hardship has paid off. Compared to other tribes, the Dinè population is massive and rising. They also have the largest reservation in the Regime. The large Dinè presence gives them a powerful political voice, helping them attain supplies from the tightfisted Regime. With acquired resources, the Dinè travel and share their traditions with the global audience. But the adaptation to colonization has a price.

Many Dinè have abandoned the traditional ways for the lifestyles, careers, and religions of the colonizers. Avoiding tradition makes the Dinè appear favorable to European employers, but distances them from their roots. Children who were born to colonized parents rarely know what it truly means to be Dinè. This separation from tradition has endangered Dinè Bizaad—the Navajo language—history from the Dinè perspective, and many religious ceremonies.

That said, practicing the traditions of forgiveness and peace hurt the Dinè. By forgiving the Regime for its wrongdoings, the Dinè portray themselves as easy targets for abuse. If the Regime is not held accountable for its malice, the Treaty of 1868 may never be fulfilled.

Perhaps citizens of the Regime should insist the Dinè receive what the Treaty of 1868 promised. While few Regime citizens have directly hurt Native Americans, most citizens passively benefit from their exploitation. Every parcel of land and acquired resource has directly been taken from the indigenous. When the oppressed choose peace and forgiveness over vengeance, the responsibility of ensuring equality belongs to all who can help. Despite appearing merciful, the Dinè will only reach Hozho when past wrongs have been made right and their survival is secured.

While adaptation to colonization appears double-sided, resilience has served the Dinè well. Most Regime tribes are unknown to the wide world. Yet the unlikely recognition of the Dinè has brought attention to the challenges Native Americans endure. In times of unparalleled hardship, broad awareness may result in quick relief.

Eventually, hard work pays off. Despite all obstacles, the resilience of the Dinè should one day result in attaining everything needed to survive and live in Hozho!

Walk in peace and beauty!

This picture displays the Navajo Nation flag over the flag of the Regime with Geronimo on it. This flag is placed in the far north of the Navajo Nation. The land beyond these flags is still occupied by the Regime despite being ancestral Dinè land.

THE REGIME'S MAINSTREAM SOCIETY

"I want it!"

"Now!"

"More!"

Far from the purgatory of reservations, towns occupying the Native American soil are filled with cacophonies of demands. The majority of these noisy complainers descended from colonizers and compose the Regime's mainstream society. Gratitude here is a rarity despite the fact that mainstream citizens usually have more resources than the empire's indigenous people. Some mainstream citizens are kind and helpful. But the majority only complain about what they lack.

In the Navajo and Hopi Nations, the blue sky curves around the expansive red earth. But the Regime's mainstream skyline looks like a dome shaped lid, a flat surface because the earth's curvature is obliterated by buildings and bridges, crowded streets, and way too many cars. Repulsive infrastructure sits beneath a gray sky that is always smoggy from the pollution of smoke-belching factories. All these things and every other "development" to the land severely devastated the earth. Yet most citizens don't care about the earth. Instead, the land is worsened by the persistent cries of "I want it! More! Now!" From citizens who are never satisfied with what they have.

Resources that are scarce on reservations abound in the mainstream society. Instead of enjoying what they have, the citizens waste resources yet always demand more. Sometimes, their fiery demands create wars so the Regime can steal from other hegemonies. Mainstream citizens don't care about the casualties. They only cry over lacking what they want.

As bad as this irresponsible behavior is, it is understandable when one realizes that mainstream citizens don't know any better. Citizens have been shielded from knowing the consequences of resource depletion. Many believe that clean water materializes from limitless supplies, not springs in the earth that need preservation.

On reservations, people learn a lot from their elders, but experience is accepted as the best teacher. In the Regime's mainstream society, people know little beyond the confines of the "unreality TV" shows constantly broadcasted.

Unreality TV is relied upon for all information. Fear of missing TV leads people to schedule their lives around the releases of new episodes.

Health detriments from inactivity are a common side effect of persistent television. However, leaders of the Regime don't care about the consequence of too much TV. On the contrary, the landlords utilize TV to prevent their citizens from knowing that the Regime is a dictatorship on indigenous soil.

Today is one of the two days that most people look forward to—the weekend. Alas, most citizens don't enjoy their weekends as much as they could as most spend the entire weekend looking at screens. One such person is a young man in a one-room dwelling, situated in a cheap apartment complex for the middle class. However, he doesn't look young. The persistent electronic entertainment has kept him up at night, leaving dark rings underneath his eyes. Junk food is the staple of the Regime's mainstream society. This man has gotten fat from eating too much of it. Like most residents of the mainstream society, he consistently chooses screen time over fresh air, resulting in a sickly pale appearance. Although he has yet to reach forty years of age, this man is already balding. Another hour is spent watching TV. This mainstream resident has been watching so much TV that he is oblivious to what day or time it is.

His mother lives across the street in an assisted living facility. She, too, is aging prematurely, and her diet of cheap junk food has made her suffer from diabetes. This man knows the Regime foods and relentless unreality TV caused his mother's poor health. Despite not wanting to end up in her situation, he continues doing things the lazy way. At least then, he won't be called unpatriotic like those thankless citizens who choose healthy foods, donate to charity, and foolishly think other countries are better than the Regime.

Generally, mainstream citizens refuse to listen to ingrates. The man in question has been more open-minded about their feedback than most men in his position. However, he refuses to join them. And wonders why should one have compassion for others when they live under a ruler that forces citizens to silently comply with their lies or endure various levels of retribution. Yet patriots insist all Regime citizens live in the best country ever. For the sake of convenience, the man in question agrees.

After all, what's the worst thing that can happen? Once again, he spends one of his two free days watching TV. In his feeble mind, all seems well until an irksome evil emerges in his life, disrupting the TV program! Nature is calling, and he must respond by pausing the show to get up off the couch and use the bathroom. How cruel can life be? He sighs in exasperation over this interruption and sluggishly walks to the bathroom in a zombie-like trance. Once inside, he gets distracted from doing his business and can't look away from what he sees in the mirror.

Oblivious to the consequences of his own actions, this person ponders questions along the lines of *Why am I fat? Why am I bald? Why do I look so much older than I really am?* Strangely, it appears that the people who have the most material items in the Regime are the most miserable. Over the years, many people have attempted to explain why this is. The man in question is incapable of figuring it out.

After finishing his business, he finds himself out of breath from his short walk back to the couch. Before continuing to watch his show, a rarity of thoughts emerges in this man's inactive mind. Deep down, he wonders if there is more to life than endless hours of laziness, junk food and TV screen time. Before he can reach any conclusions, TV noises and a clatter in the neighbor's apartment distract him from thinking, and he quickly forgets the thoughts he just had. This man is one of many who are trapped in this cycle of meaningless existence. Little does he know that soon, everything will change, and missing a TV program will be the least of his worries.

THE BLUE KACHINA

While mainstream citizens overindulge on genetically modified amber waves of grain, the Hopi enjoy satisfying sustainable meals of squash, beans, and melons.

But maize is their traditional staple crop and holds an important place in Hopi history.[1] According to the Hopi creation story, the Kachinas offered each Native American culture a type of maize to sustain themselves. Most chose maize that grows easily. In lieu of easier options, the Hopis chose short-stalk maize, which is difficult to cultivate and requires around-the-clock care. Hopis surmounted the rigors of cultivating it and diversified the tricky maize into every color of the rainbow. Each Hopi maize variety is sacred and used only for a specific ceremonial purpose or food recipe. In years when it fails to grow, the corresponding ceremonies are canceled.[2]

The diversity of Hopi maize.

European missionaries have challenged the sanctity Hopi people attribute to maize since their first contact with these Native Americans. But today, one short, wiry, middle-aged farmer named Kotutuwa Nawasha is preserving its salience. He consistently grows multiple varieties of maize in the Nawasha farming plot in a dugout below the third mesa. This agricultural vocation was inspired by a lineage of farmers and a traditional Hopi upbringing.

As a child, Kotutuwa always rose early to weed maize fields under the cool violet sky of dawn. When the yellow sunrise swept across the sky, Kotutuwa breakfasted and prepared for school. Only when the sun was in full force would he trek the seven miles along dusty, unpaved roads to school and study a Regime-approved Eurocentric curriculum.

Kotutuwa was a strong student despite his rigorous farming responsibilities. He was also the only person in his graduating class at Hopi High School to attend college. At Cornell University, Kotutuwa avidly absorbed everything in the field of agricultural engineering. He agreed with most of what was taught but not everything.

For example, Kotutuwa's lessons centered around genetically modifying plants to grow in different climates. This latest development in European farming seeks to provide farmers with a steady income giving consumers consistent products. Both farmers and consumers appear to get what they want from these genetically modified crops.

In millennia prior, Hopis learned forcing plants to fit the land led to weakened crops and blight. Beyond blight, the Hopi believe that plants have souls and feelings. Farmers are the plants' parents because they nurture them from seedlings through harvest. As parents, Hopis sing to their plants while approaching because they believe it benefits the crops' emotional well-being and encourages them to grow in height and love each day. At Cornell, Kotutuwa was told this sentiment was lunacy and not scientific. But Hopis believed that forcing plants to grow in undesired climates backfire on the farmer when it should, say, disappoint the farmer.

Yet a large intersection exists between both Hopi and European farming practices. Both Hopis and corporations desire high crop yields. As an astute student, Kotutuwa diligently explored ways to enhance crop yield both on the mesas and in commercial farms. Some of Kotutuwa's ideas impressed his professors and made him prominently stand out among the hundreds of students in attendance.

The brilliance of Kotutuwa's Native American beauty further classified him in large lecture halls. The typical ivy league student in the early 2000s was European. Unlike most students at Cornell, Kotutuwa's beautiful copper skin radiated across campus like the sun at daybreak. Being Hopi short, on average, Kotutuwa was an inch shorter than European women. He was usually the shortest person in all his classes. His long raven black hair draped around his lean, muscular torso dark bangs frame kind milk chocolate-colored eyes.

Kotutuwa was most professors' first indigenous student. They warmly welcomed him and also strove to learn everything about the Hopi people and their farming practices. Teachers at Cornell were impressed by Hopi wisdom and asked Kotutuwa if he would share it with everyone. This led to Kotutuwa getting paid to lecture European peers on indigenous farming.

Kotutuwa would present his lectures while wearing his leather skirt and woven poncho. He instructed, "We Hopi never water our maize because we live in a dry desert with limited water. Seeds are planted six inches deep to help them reach groundwater. Our maize fields are directly beneath cliffs. During the rainy season, water tumbles off these cliffs and accumulates in the maize patches giving us a free water reservoir! Our maize will absorb this water all year. To ensure our maize utilized every last drop of water, it is left on the stalk until the stalk turns brown. We weed our crops only by hand to ensure that all of our crops are well taken care of."[3]

After graduating from Cornell, Kotutuwa made large sums of money working with agribusiness firms. For the first time in his life, Kotutuwa had material pleasures on demand. However,

Kotutuwa always felt empty inside and longed for his family. His heart yearned for the mesas, but Kotutuwa had resolved to impact the colonized world after graduation. These ambitions changed twelve years ago with a phone call from his grandmother, Naha.

At that time, Kotutuwa's parents were driving their old, dilapidated car to Tuba City. Most roads on the Hopi reservation are unpaved and remotely desolate. Such was the road Kotutuwa's parents traveled. Unfortunately, a rickety car on a winding, washboard road full of potholes made for a bad combination. During a beautiful spring drive through fields full of colorful flowers and budding maize, a cassette tape fell from the dashboard to the car's metal floor.

The loud clank distracted the driver, Kotutuwa's father. Reflexively, Mr. Nawasha lunged, attempting to retrieve it, while continuing to drive. Kotutuwa's mother also hunched over to help her husband retrieve the tape. Neither person was watching the road during the tape search. After recovering the tape, Mr. Nawasha looked up and saw a sheep directly in his path. Instinctively, Mr. Nawasha jerked the car's wheel to the right as hard as he could. He meant to brake but accidentally accelerated. The car sped out of control, flying into a ravine. It crash-landed, exploded into flames, and instantly killed both of Kotutuwa's parents.

Traditionally, the eldest Hopi daughter inherits all land and belongings. As an only child, Kotutuwa was the sole heir of the Nawasha farming plot, incentivizing him to return home. Furthermore, his Grandmother Naha became deeply traumatized by the sudden loss of her daughter and son-in-law. Her dark hair quickly began to gray from the shock, despite her sepia face remaining youthful. When Naha tearfully called Kotutuwa to tell him, "We are the sole survivors of this family," Kotutuwa altered his ambitions and left the conveniences of mainstream society.

Kotutuwa's homecoming mirrored the Hopi legacy of taking a rigorous path when offered an easy route. After years of indulgent mainstream society, Kotutuwa had to readjust to traveling miles for water and groceries and other basic necessities. But the rigors of Hopi life create strong and resilient people. Perseverance has benefited the Hopi, and it will continue strengthening Kotutuwa. Indefatigable tenacity is always an asset to those who challenge European domination. Soon, everything will change for the worst, and resilience will be needed more than ever.

Right now, Kotutuwa is finishing his farming for the day because dusk begins obscuring the limitless red land. He has been back on the mesa, working the land for several years. This gives him thickly calloused hands, which he wipes on the coveralls over his muscular body. Yet he remains youthful and optimistic in spirit despite possessing a tough exterior.

As the evening darkens, Kotutuwa ascends an old wooden ladder to exit his maize field dugout. One can see constellations and galaxies without an influx of artificial light.

Small white stars begin to flicker under the veil of night. Kotutuwa studies the stars above him for clues on what the future holds. Out of nowhere, the stars change, and Kotutuwa sees something appalling. Horrified, Kotutuwa loses control of his body and almost falls backward into his maize field. After the paralyzing shock passes, Kotutuwa runs to his rusty, maroon 1980s pickup truck, and speeds to the village of Oraibi.

Kotutuwa hurries to warn villagers about the stars. But when he arrives, the entire village is already standing outside their adobe homes, the inn, and the Hopi Cultural Center. Oraibi doesn't have any streetlights, and tonight, there is no need for any. Everything and everyone is brightly glowing from the blue star. Light radiates off of everyone's dumbfounded faces. Chins point to the horizon as all eyes are focused upwards, making the Hopi's deep dark eyes look blue and unaware of Kotutuwa's arrival.

Kotutuwa spots his grandmother Naha in the crowd. He joins her and says, "The blue star!"

Naha keeps her maple-syrup-colored eyes upward and comments, "I never thought I would see this in my lifetime. We were warned that it was coming. For seven years, children have claimed to see blue Kachinas during the Snake Dance Ceremony. Still, all we can do is predict. But we never know where the Kachinas are until they reveal themselves. Now we know the Blue Kachina is returning to earth. A great destruction will follow, and then we'll be in the fifth world. Let this sight serve as a warning sign for all of us to finish whatever unfinished business we may have. All wrongs must be made right before it's too late. And soon, it *will* be too late. For now, more than ever, it is of great importance that we live our lives in the purest of ways."

Kotutuwa silently nods, accepting this solemn truth.

They stand together in silence, joining the growing congregation of Hopis mesmerized by ethereal blue light. No one knows what will come next. But they do know that it will be torturous, and only the pure of heart will survive.

THE DETECTIVE OF THE DEAD

Each year in the Regime, a sick season occurs when many citizens become ill. Fortunately, the affluence of the Regime has resulted in the creation of vaccines to prevent diseases. But this year's illness will be different. The outcome will change the world.

Two weeks ago, as if on schedule, the sick season began. But this viral strain seems stronger and different than last year. Elderly and the infirm citizens have quickly become bedridden and hospitalized, requiring machine assistance to breathe. Medical facilities are rapidly running out of beds, equipment, and personnel to treat the rapidly increasing numbers of sick people.

Yesterday was the first sick season induced death. The victim's autopsy is currently being performed in an overly air-conditioned and well-lit room. The medical examiner about to conduct the autopsy has a sickly, pale complexion as if her body has prepared for studying the dreadful disease. Obnoxiously bright florescent lights unpleasantly accentuate her ill appearance. Ready to begin the autopsy, she creakily opens the stubborn steel drawer containing the corpse.

X-rays taken of the cadaver's chest reveal a buildup of fluid in the lungs. Bafflement befuddles the medical examiner when comparing the x-rays to the corpse's case file and medical records. Many pulmonary ailments cause this type of death by internal drowning. However, the victim under examination never displayed symptoms corresponding to any disease known to cause this death.

She then extracts blood and fluid from the corpse's intercostals. More conclusive tests are conducted. Her results were logged into the Center for Disease Control database, which catalogs all known diseases.

There are no matches or similar diseases to the virus which killed the first victim. This discovery is startling because it means that there is a brand-new entity on the horizon. It eerily looks like a crown when viewed under an electron microscope. The examiner mails these results to scientists around the world. Together they eagerly try to unravel this mysterious crown-shaped virus.

Thousands have already died because the disease is severely contagious. Yesterday, scientists were finally able to identify the culprit disease. Now people obsess over the crown virus's mysterious origins

Feebleminded mainstream citizens fail to understand the severity of the crown virus's symptoms. Likewise, they have zero tolerance for uncertainty and cope by clinging to what they do know: patriotism. Zealous patriots believe that the Regime is under attack and must be defended. Suspicious circumstances enshroud politics between the Regime and another country called the Middle Kingdom. Influenced by the negativity of these politics, citizens of the Regime blame the Middle Kingdom for the disease.

This blame seems illogical, but it is encouraged by current events. Despite having the highest population density in today's world, the Middle Kingdom has the lowest crown virus infection rate. Surprisingly, the Regime has the world's highest crown infection and death rate despite its smaller population. Scientists unintentionally egg on patriotic sentiment by referring the crown virus as a foreign entity. Unlike past years, researchers express a newfound difficulty in creating cures for the crown virus.

Steeped in mystery, little is known about this latest disease. What is known is that the illness acts like an impressive air force that attacks tracheas like kamikazes. Unlike the original kamikazes who were given direct targets to hit with strict rules enforced, these infections lack rules and regulations. Every person is endangered by the plague's cavalry. The swift mobility of the illness ought to prompt the president to fortify citizens. Instead, the landlord of the Regime favors money over their citizen's health and well-being. People are forced to work despite the infiltrating plague.

Scientists, unlike the landlord, attempt to fight back and create virus prevention protocols. People are now encouraged to wear cloth face masks to quell airborne attacks. Further protocol encourages people to stand six feet apart. This will slow contagion by preventing the disease from raiding people. Gloves are also encouraged to prevent oblivious humans from transporting crown virus weaponry, unintentionally equipping the disease to launch more attacks.

Unfortunately, the president won't mandate the virus prevention protocols. Many citizens listen to their state landlords and disregard the scientists. In particular, citizens claim that the new "social distancing" paradigm is a revocation of liberty. Tensions grow because the president refuses to listen to scientists and encourages civil unrest from citizens who only care about themselves.

Two months have passed since the completion of the first victim's autopsy. Each following day is marked by a rising death toll. Like a figurative royal pain, the plague kills its victims slowly and painfully. Due to its crown shape, one could suggest that this virus is a literal royal pain. Despite the impact of the disease, ignorant citizens remain undeterred and loyal to their selfish ways. But if ashes are to ashes what dust is to dust, could a crown virus act as a crown of politics? No one knows the origins of this crown virus. But what if the origin is where one would least expect? What if this crown virus bears heirs to a new throne for a new world? Or what if the crown shape of the virus signifies the crown of god(s) restoring order to the American continents?

A GATHERING OF NATIONS

Mainstream citizens mourn the loss of frivolities during a pandemic. But Native Americans panic frantically because death by disease appears to be their most common death sentence in the Regime dictatorship.

To make matters worse, the crown virus targets people with diabetes and hypertension. Out of all ethnic groups in the Regime, Native Americans have the highest rate per capita of diabetes and hypertension, making them the most vulnerable. The seemingly doomed fate of Native Americans is compounded by the fact that hospitals on tribal lands lack sufficient resources and personnel. Adding to the attacks against the First Nations is the fact that one in three Native Americans lives in poverty. Poverty puts people at a disadvantage during pandemics. People who can't afford virus prevention products die.

Poverty is only worsening. Tribal businesses act as the vagus nerve to their tribe's economy. A lack of customers from the pandemic forces businesses to furlough workers. The severe poverty on reservations is becoming widespread penury.

The life of indigenous people in the Regime has always rested in a precarious balance between survival and annihilation. Plague is shifting this balance into a perilous position. Hoping to survive another epidemic, the Hopi and Navajo Nations will meet online to develop a warpath tomorrow.

The red sandstone peaks of the Navajo Nation's southern region shimmer in the waning autumn sun. Cold gusts of mountain air stir loose soil into dancing spirals across these high desert summits. Window Rock, a large spherical hole near the apex, funnels the wind to the valley below. The valley lays beneath the mountain's shadow into which the cold breeze drives fallen leaves across streets full of potholes. The leaves settle against the Navajo tribal government office and lay motionless.

Inside the office, tribal council leaders silently stare at the large image projected from a computer. Sharp and solemn, the thirty members continue to wait for the Hopi to join the virtual conference. Navajos, who refer to themselves as Dinè, are known for possessing exceptional patience. However, recent circumstances have challenged their fortitude.

Many Dinè have succumbed to the raging crown virus pandemic and the Navajo Nation clinic is struggling to help everyone. Feeling immensely threatened by disease, the Dinè have abandoned their easygoing ways.

Frustrated of waiting, Tony Largo, the Navajo Nation president, stands to address the council. He says, "We agreed with the Hopi that this meeting would take place an hour ago. Can I have the approval to remind them of our meeting?" Everyone nods in agreement. The Hopi Nation is again summoned through the computer, but they do not answer.

*****

Crisp air blows through the recently harvested maize fields, which are now full of tilted brown stalks. The land begins to ascend, and traditional homes are embedded in a cliff's shadow. The waning autumn sun shines over the third mesa, highlighting a small traditional adobe that houses the Hopi tribal government and overlooks the valley below.

Louis Loloma, the Hopi Nation's president, has gathered the Hopi tribal government here to start a dialogue with the Navajo Nation regarding the pandemic. The only light in this small one-room building is from the computer screen projected on to a dark clay wall. Gray smoke from burnt cedar fills the room with a calming scent for the tense meeting. Suddenly the spiritual atmosphere of the room is interrupted by an electronic *Ding!* Everyone in attendance jumps—startled out of their meditative reverie state—

and sees "Incoming Video Call from Navajo Nation" message displayed on the clay wall.

Emory, a short, wiry, spry Hopi elder, sighs while ambling up to the computer. The glow from the computer reveals the fatigue on her sleep-deprived face. Despite her exhausted appearance, Emory seems energetic and mentally alert.

Nervously tugging on her long gray braids, Emory projects her voice to the assembled group and firmly says, "Our neighbors are ready. Is everyone here ready to begin?"

Heads nod in silent agreement.

"All right. I'll return the Navajo's call."

The Dinè quickly answer the Hopi's video call, and greetings are exchanged. Previous information about the disease reaching and infecting the large Navajo Nation has spread fear throughout the small, encircled Hopi Nation.

Eager for updates, Louis Loloma asks of the Dinè, "How are you guys doing?"

Tony Largo uneasily takes a deep breath before answering, "I would be lying to you if I told you that I wasn't scared of what is happening. All of us natives have been through many pandemics before. But this disease is the worst we've seen." His voice breaks while tears run down his round, full cheeks.

Another Dinè council member steps in for president Largo and continues, "All of us Dinè and Hopi know how easily this crown virus spreads and that it has penetrated our Navajo Nation. Already our hospital staff struggles to help assist our ailing residents, and the sick season has just begun. How are you holding up, dear Hopi friends?"

Naha, Kotutuwa's grandmother, answers, "So far, so good. But we fear things will get worse."

After gaining composure and wiping the remaining tears from his face, Tony Largo suggests, "Yes. We must talk about that. I want us to come together and develop a warpath against this disease."

The Hopi president, Mr. Loloma, admits, "Securing virus prevention supplies is essential for survival. Even before the pandemic, our long distance from stores puts supplies out of easy reach. Even if we weren't so isolated, would it be wise to expose ourselves to the world?" No one has an answer, but everyone knows they should consider a nationwide quarantine.

Curiously, Louis Loloma asks the Dinè, "What is the biggest threat you face?"

It is hard to identify the worst thing when one is given nothing but hardship.

After moments of silent contemplation, a Navajo council member laments, "We have a lot to worry about. Few homes have running water. Extended families live together which can spread contamination. Many residents are at high risk for the illness due to diabetes and hypertension. Also, our tribal hospitals don't have the supplies they need to adequately aid the sick people."

Hopis reflect upon their neighbor's strife.

In a gruff voice, Mr. Loloma sadly agrees. "We face a lot of similar challenges. But we Hopis are even more removed from the world."

Both tribes fall silent.

The oldest elder in the Hopi Nation warns, "Our biggest challenge has yet to come. All tribes have had to fight for existence since the arrival of Europeans. Thus far, we have surprised everyone by outlasting both disease and slaughter. Yes, we've survived every battle thus far. But we have also lost something in each trial. If we survive this pandemic, what more will we lose?"

Tony Largo clears his throat and confidently says, "We will lose less if we work together. Let's team up and help each other survive the plague."

Silence is the Hopi's response. They reflect on the Dinè repeatedly encroaching Hopi land. Both tribes have teamed up in the past. Despite agreeing to work together, the Dinè have historically shortchanged the Hopi. Yet survival of both tribes is threatened. Therefore, one must choose their allies wisely. Of the two things Hopis associate with their populous neighbors, the first is unfairness. Second is the uncanny ability of the Dinè in securing resources from the Regime. How rare it is for the Regime to help any Native Americans. Yet the Dinè usually get assistance most tribes wouldn't dream of. Fortunately for the Hopi, these astute victors reside next door.

Sentimentalism is ended abruptly when a young Hopi named Rasa questions, "How would we benefit from working with you Navajos?"

Also aware of their past broken agreements, the Dinè balk at the question.

Mr. Largo diplomatically answers, "If we work together, we will have greater success in gaining global awareness of our suffering. We can share the help we receive."

The Hopis do not entirely trust the Dinè. Yet they are not completely distrusting of the Dinè either.

Rasa returns a new question to the Dinè: "How will we get help?"

The Navajo tribal government had planned a solution before proposing it to the Hopi. So Mr. Largo quickly continues, "On the internet, we can start a charity fund for ourselves. That platform will enable people from around the world to donate money to us. The donations we receive will secure water and the virus prevention products for residents in both nations."

This plan seems sensible to the Hopi. But skepticism remains.

Naha asks, "What if we get nothing from charity?"

The Navajo Nation treasurer, Annie, responds, "Following virus prevention protocol, our Navajo Nation will establish a mandatory quarantine for all residents. Perhaps you Hopi can do the same? At least then, we are taking action to limit the spread of disease."

Sinquah, the Hopi treasurer, answers, "I believe both nations should implement a reservation-wide quarantine. Especially since so many of our residents are at high risk of illness. Now, if we do acquire resources, how will they be divided?"

Annie, the Navajo Nation treasurer, replies, "Let's begin by naming our fund. I propose the Navajo Hopi COVID-19 Relief Fund."

Hopi council heads nod approval, and so the president, Louis Loloma, advises the Navajo of the Hopi agreement.

Tony Largo continues by reminding the Hopi, "We Navajo have a larger nation, so we should attain the bulk of the funds."

In defiance, Sinquah quickly objects, "It would be fair to divide donations equally."

Mr. Largo counters, "We Dinè will probably be hit harder than you Hopi. Our tribal council is thinking that based on the two size differences, the Hopi Nation should receive 25 percent of all donations. That, of course, would mean my Navajo Nation would get 75 percent. Remember that we have the largest tribe in the Regime. Comparatively, all Hopi Nation residents form 15 percent of the Navajo Nation's population. To help our residents, we will need a greater share from more resources."

For the next course of action, the Hopi Nation disconnects from the video call. A vote for the allocation of donations is conducted, and the Hopi agree to allow their Navajo neighbors 75 percent of all donations even though the Hopi could foretell being shortchanged in this latest agreement with the Navajo.

Fortunately for the Dinè, the Hopi are fair and reasonable. They also acknowledge that the Navajo Nation is much larger and less isolated. Hopis also predict that the Navajo Nation will be hit harder than their own nation. A vote for the allocation of donations was conducted, and the Hopi agreed to allow their neighbors' 75 percent of all donations. Resuming the video call, the Hopi president informed the Dinè that they would acquiesce to the Dinè terms.

QUARANTINE PROTESTS

Fortunately, most cities in the mainstream society have sufficient virus prevention products and adequate hospitals. Unlike the destitute tribal nations, people who reside in the mainstream society have a decent shot at surviving the pandemic. However, these ignorant people destroy their own survival. For their challenge is not a lack of resources; rather, it is a refusal to take the crown virus pandemic seriously.

While tribal nations brace for annihilation, selfish people in the mainstream society mourn the pandemic-related restrictions for pleasures of the flesh such as eating out, the cinema, or watching live sports games. Selfish people refuse to acknowledge thousands of fellow citizens who perished in anguish from the crown virus.

Aggravatingly, for the medical community, feebleminded citizens propagate the crown virus and strengthen its reign by refusing to follow virus prevention protocols. Benevolent healthcare workers have long since become fatigued and overworked, and some have gotten sick and died from the rising plague. But patriots don't seem to care about the fatigued medical staff or the many lost loved ones from the rising plague.

The Regime's tradition of reckless egocentric behavior seems inconceivable in this current plight. However, ignorance and greed are the Regime's cornerstone.

Before the Regime became a self-sufficient country, it began as a colony for a greedy country known as the Crown. George Number Three, the Crown's reigning landlord at that time, decided to further his worldly exploits and add the North American continent to his kingdom. Tenants, the commoners to George Number

Three, implemented genocidal tactics, and colonists wiped out the entire American ecosystem on the king's behalf. As compensation for executing George's dirty deeds, American colonists were given military protection and supplies to sustain themselves. Out of lust for more privileges and added pleasures, colonists started a war and ultimately usurped the Crown.

After the colonists won the bloody war they waged against the Crown, George Number Three signed the Regime's birth certificate which is known as the Declaration of Independence. Living in a country teeming with unexploited resources caused the Regime's first mainstream citizen's selfishness to explode. In the following centuries, descendants of the colonizers who usurped the Crown have executed countless wars and land thefts on other nations across the earth. Trillions of people have been displaced by American greed.

Fortunately, today's complaints are not about the Regime's desire for foreign invasions.

Instead, the ignorant Regime citizens protest how unfair virus prevention protocols are. Following in the footsteps of their colonial ancestors, angry citizens make their frustrations known to all. At hospitals, the epicenters for valiantly trying to quash this disease, mainstream complaints are blatantly broadcasted.

A tall building with a soapy gray color overlooks the multitudes of mainstream streets. An observer looking down from above might think this building is hosting a fun event because of all the cars parked outside. For why else would people eagerly transform busy and flowing city streets into disorderly packed parking lots?

Surprisingly, this building is not surrounded by crowds attending a fun center. It is actually one of the busiest hospitals in the Regime. Before the pandemic, this hospital was famous for having entire floors dedicated to specific medical specialties. Current circumstances have altered its mission. Physicians with niche specialties are rerouting their forte to care for the growing number of patients inflicted with the crown virus. Despite being one of the best equipped facilities in the world, this hospital is failing to compete with the spreading viral nightmare.

To prevent the disease from escaping the hospital boundaries, health care staff workers and patients are the only ones allowed entry. Altruistic nurses have graciously offered their personal mobile devices so the isolated and dying patients can say their final goodbyes to their families.

As dire as the atmosphere in the hospital is, the mood is worsened outside. Angry about having their liberties limited through virus prevention protocols, mainstream citizens illogically attack hospitals. They have purposefully parked cars in close proximity so the surroundings streets have become impassible parking lots. Obnoxiously and continuously the honked horns overpower the hum of electricity from other buildings. Pedestrian protestors squish their bodies between cars and bellow insults at exhausted nurses who are risking their own health to save humanity from crown disease and death.

Undeterred by the crown virus, protestors chant, "This is the Regime! Land of the Free! If you want communism, go to the Middle Kingdom!" Little do these angry protestors know that soon, they will pay the price for their own greed.

* * * * *

Nearby, a few miles away from the soapy gray hospital is an assisted living center. Residents of this center are particularly vulnerable to the plague due to their advanced age and weakened health disposition. Today, someone's mother who has diabetes has been taken hostage by the crown virus.

Fortunately, she lives in a metropolitan area with efficient first responders. Assisted living center staff have dialed the Regime's emergency number earlier this morning when this sick woman first expressed difficulty breathing. Within ten minutes of the call, paramedics arrived to perform their benevolent, and in this pandemic, increasingly dangerous duty.

Emergency oxygen was deployed to help her survive the quick ride to the hospital. But since the crown virus initially attacks the lungs, emergency oxygen is constantly needed to aid the sick. It is now in high demand and cautiously rationed. Limited oxygen only sustains people until a ventilator becomes necessary. Fortunately, the hospital is only a few miles away because its proximity provides the greatest hope in this challenging circumstance.

After the rapid ambulance commute through the city, an unusual obstacle emerges. Cars are parked so tightly together that the ambulance can't drive through to reach the hospital. This peril is created by quarantine protestors who are now jeopardizing people's lives. Minutes that feel like hours pass while emergency oxygen plummets and the victim's lungs weaken. After much honking and blaring of sirens, the angry mob relents and allows the vehicle through. The hospital trauma center is finally reached!

A thin ray of hope lies on the horizon when this woman is lifted out of the ambulance and taken into the hospital. Regrettably, as her gurney is wheeled through the hospital's doors, she exhales the last of her emergency oxygen ration. Before healthcare workers can wheel her to a ventilator, her heart flatlines.

If only mainstream citizens cared about others. Then this untimely death could have been avoided. Today, someone lost their mother because citizens are devoted to avarice. This death is a rude awakening for the woman's son who will go on to achieve extraordinary things.

After their shift ends, weary hospital staff is angrily confronted by the mobs about activity in the trauma center. Ignorant people verbally attack frustrated workers. The mob thinks that they are protecting their constitutional freedoms from being tread upon. But if one reaps what one sows, what is the ultimate price for their selfishness?

THE PANDEMIC AND
THE DINÈ PART 1

After launching the Navajo Hopi COVID-19 Relief Fund, the Navajo Nation tribal government established temporary laws for a nationwide quarantine. One new law asks residents not to leave the Navajo Nation. Since most residents are employed off the reservation, this law is hard to enforce. However, unemployment and poverty are rising with the domination of disease. A side effect of rising unemployment is reduced travel off the reservation. This, in turn, reduces the crown virus's chances of infecting the Dinè. That said, unemployment renders vulnerable people destitute.

Many Dinè are using spirituality to cope with the new virus prevention protocols. Elders, the tribe's keepers of oral history, are particularly vulnerable to the dangers this plague poses. As such, this disease not only threatens people's lives but the Dinè historical and traditional way of life. To remind residents about the dire consequences this pandemic has for elders, the tribal council puts up signs warning everyone to "Protect our elders. Stay home."

Beyond posting signs, virus prevention accountability is hard to encourage. The Dinè traditionally operate as a matrilineal society with land and belongings passed from mother to daughter. The Dinè matriarchy governs everything from inheritance to marriages and family living arrangements. Following matrimony, a man moves into his wife's family *Hogan*. Inside a *Hogan*, the traditional Dinè home, husbands live with a matriarch's extended family. Therefore, elders who are vulnerable to the virus live in multigenerational dwellings with young people who might transmit it from hauling water or from farming in close proximity to other potentially infected people.

Another downside to the good-intentioned virus prevention protocols is the effect it has on traditional practices. Different seasons correspond to public ceremonies that have all been canceled to curb the disease. Dinè neighbors frequently team up and gather resources such as firewood and edible plants on the reservation. This neighborly teaming up has been restricted to social distance.

People begin feeling helpless due to the rising poverty and confines of quarantine. Animosity is bred from this massive detention and chaos ensues. A culture where people historically worked together to achieve a common goal has been uprooted. The Dinè begin to violate their own traditional ethics by resenting and envying each other.

Navajo Nation residents begin stealing vehicles, sheep, and other precious commodities from their friends and neighbors. As thievery increases, crown virus cases in the Navajo Nation rise. This trend confuses the tribal council because virus prevention protocols get stricter by the day. Perhaps the disease is punishing the Dinè for turning on each other instead of getting organized amid chaos.

Outside the Navajo Nation, across the Regime, every overpopulated and usually affluent city is besieged by disease. They are unable to curtail the crown virus, and the victim count rises each day. The Regime's towering buildings and grand infrastructures are morphing into hospitals and cemeteries. In this pandemic, Native Americans, who compose 1 percent of the population, have the highest crown virus death rate. In a country succumbing to sickness and death, the Navajo Nation has the highest crown virus infection rate despite being much smaller in size and in population than many Regime states.

In response to the viral devastation wreaking havoc throughout the Regime, which is now overwhelming the Navajo Nation, Dinè elder and medicine man, Jim Sweetwater, takes to his computer. Jim's long gray hair is always wrapped in the traditional Dinè bun, and a colorful headband is worn over his forehead, resting above his peppered eyebrows.

A short, stout man with bulky muscles, he is known for defiantly using European ways to preserve his culture. His most recent act of defiance is creating a YouTube channel run by his grandson, Joe. On YouTube, Jim and Joe share traditional Dinè practices so that many people can benefit from them. Unlike Jim, most Dinè elders distance themselves from technology because they believe it is the latest threat to traditions.

After a lifetime of being kissed by the sun, Jim has beautiful sandstone-colored skin. Known to radiate joy the way the sun radiates light, Jim is a jovial man who laughs as much as most people breathe. While many people monger fear of the unknown, Jim takes a lighthearted approach to most things. These endearing traits are evidenced by the twinkles in his wide-set, coal-colored eyes and the wrinkles that highlight the permanent smile on his face.

But today is different. Jim's usual upbeat countenance is soured by recent events. Disgust clouds Jim's face as he adjusts his turquoise bead necklace underneath the collar of his yellow button-down shirt. Jim's grandson Joe looks just like the high school version of himself with the exception of a small red flared birthmark on his upper-right cheekbone. This birthmark has earned Joe the nickname Redwing. After setting up his camera, Redwing hesitantly asks grandpa, "Are you ready?"

Today, the duo will share a warning and somber wake-up call for all. Neither person wants to deliver this message, but it must be done. In response to Redwing's question, Jim lowers his voice and grumbles, "As ready as I'll ever be." Jim grabs his white-yellow-red-and-black-striped story stick and positions his thick barreled chest in front of a traditional Dinè tapestry. Redwing turns the camera on and announces, "We are going live in," and begins counting backward from four in Dinè Bizad: "*dį́į́', táá', naaki, t'ááłá'í.*" A beeping noise signals that the recording has just begun. Jim extends his somber expression straight into the camera lens and delivers his message:

> It saddens me that so many of our people have left the old ways and suffer because of it. I hear that people are stealing livestock, horse trailers, water hauling trailers, cars, and even family pets from their fellow Dinè. But these things don't belong to you. You didn't earn any of these things. The families you stole them from worked hard to earn those belongings. This thieving behavior saddens me because it proves that our youth have abandon morality. Future generations will only suffer because of this abandoning of what is right.
>
> Our Holy People have forbidden us Dinè from stealing anything. The consequences of stealing are severe. The Holy People are kind and forgiving. But you must undo your wrongs to receive their forgiveness. Our purpose as Dinè is to find peace, joy, confidence, and happiness in everything we do. But when you do evil things like steal, lie, and cheat, the Holy People will punish you by making you feel the opposite of peace, joy, confidence, and happiness.
>
> You need to return everything you have stolen immediately! It doesn't matter how small or large the item you stole is. Stealing is stealing regardless of size and value. Even if you think what you stole was insignificant, you and your relatives will still be punished for your theft.
>
> We live in a world where our way of life has been ridiculed and many people have tried to destroy us. But we have no control over what other people do to us. We do, however, have control over how we act. So what saddens me

the most is when we Dinè choose to act like colonizers with dishonesty and stealing.

Foreigners have ridiculed our traditional family structure for centuries. They claim that we only need a small, nuclear family. But the consequences of our actions still apply to every single one of our clan relatives, the true Dinè family. So when you go about your life, think about your family before you do anything. What you do impacts them too.

I know that this bad behavior is happening because many people are hurting right now. I hear about families losing their jobs and people who are getting sick and dying from the crown virus. This is not an excuse for bad behavior. We create the worst pain by hurting people who are already suffering. And the pain we give other people will come back to hurt us and our relatives.

The Holy People have instructed us to never talk bad about any circumstance but to instead find peace, joy, confidence, and happiness in every part of our life. This "no talking badly" rule applies to the pandemic too. So stop stealing and stop disobeying the virus prevention protocols. Our people have survived wars, starvation, and pandemics before. But we only survived all those things because we helped each other get through them. We would have never gotten to where we are today if we had a history of acting the way many of you are currently acting.

I encourage you to help your relatives and fellow Dinè. We must all adhere to our moral traditions for the good of everyone. Use your time in quarantine not by doing bad things, but as a time to enjoy that which brings you peace, joy, happiness, and confidence. After I upload this video, I will be conducting the Evil Way Ceremony to get rid of the evil behavior in this world.

My elders were always cautious when they conducted this ceremony, and they never liked talking about it because the Evil Way Ceremony calls upon the Holy People to directly rid the world of all evil. I myself do not like to take part in this ritual because we should be resolving our own conflicts. But more importantly, I do not wish for anyone to experience the Holy People's wrath. When this Ceremony is completed, anyone who has been evil will have suffered a harsh punishment. Like them, I have always waited for the worst things to happen so that I know I can't avoid conducting this ceremony. In this time of chaos and bad behavior, I know that the Evil Way Ceremony must be conducted to restore order.

Please remember that whatever you are going through right now, it will not last forever. You reap what you sow. A time will come when the good-hearted are rewarded and those with evil intentions are punished. Let this be a warning for you who watch this. Choose what you do wisely.

Another beep signals that the recording is complete. Redwing turns his camera off and uploads the video to YouTube while his grandpa is grabbing all the suitcases and exiting the family *Hogan*. When the upload is complete, Jim and Redwing exit their family *Hogan*, inherited by Jim's eldest daughter after his wife's passing. They had packed plenty of supplies for a ceremony that will take months to complete, specifically pouches of sacred corn pollen because it evokes the Holy People and can be used to call upon ancestors for guidance.

THE HOPI AND THE VIRUS PART 1

Severe contagion enables the crown virus to wreak havoc across the world. Densely populated regions are usually more affected than the isolated ones because the crown virus spreads easily in crowds of people. Of all isolated regions in our world, the Hopi Nation is quite desolate.

In fact, Hopis have always endured unique challenges because of the distance between them and the rest of the world. Yet this isolation which stifles their economic stability and global recognition enables Hopi traditions to endure and survive. An argument could be made that despite ruthless occupation, the Hopi's true success is the antiquity of their traditions, which have been verbally passed across generations. Hopi success becomes more apparent when comparing them to neighboring, less isolated tribes whose traditions are vanishing.

The Hopis hoped that the physical distance separating them from the rest of the world would at least shield them from the plague. Instead, the virus has infected the surrounding Navajo Nation endangering the Hopis to disease. Unfortunately, distance has failed to protect the Hopi from disease. Yet ironically, distance impedes the arrival of financial and medical relief.

Desperate for survival, the Hopi and Navajo tribal governments have teamed up to beg the president of the Regime for relief. As usual, empty promises are the Regime's response. Therefore, they implore the Bureau of Indian Affairs (BIA) for help. Unfortunately, the BIA, which is responsible for all Native Americans, is overwhelmed by similar cries for help from all 574 tribes. The crown virus wreaks havoc upon the populous cities of the mainstream society, has completely devastated tribal nations.

In this unusual time, Hopis look to the TV for guidance on how descendants of colonizers and nonindigenous racial minorities are coping. Is it in the Hopi's best interest to protest quarantine like those on TV? The Hopi tribal government has worked to prevent people from protesting or gathering in large groups. Inspired by the Navajo, Hopis are now under strict curfew and disallowed from leaving the reservation. The tribal government fears what will happen if the Hopi residents who outnumber them choose to protest like those shown rebelling on TV.

After all, the Hopi have succumbed to the influence of Europeans before. Despite the ongoing fight for cultural survival, Hopi ceremonies, traditions, and even words of their language have been lost with time under the Regime's reign. With civil unrest mounting, the Hopi tribal government fears that peace will be the next abandoned tradition. Civil unrest is unpleasant and takes a toll on law enforcement and the general population everywhere. But the Hopi government is ill-equipped for a rebellion of any kind. Any act of civil disobedience can usurp the tribal government's sovereignty. Who knows what would follow?

To prevent chaos, solutions must be devised quickly, yet positive outcomes seem impossible in this worsening world.

Winter, the climax of the Regime's sick season, has arrived. Until the seasons change, death and disease will only increase. Cold wind blows red sand into the sad eyes of the hungry Hopis. But in this bleak time, sand is the least of their worries. High desert winter taunts Hopi residents by icing streets and freezing the air they breathe. Dry powdery snow smothers everything in a blanket of white, and people accept that they can't utilize frozen resources. Hopi Nation residents rely on fires for warmth because few homes have electricity. While there are *Wi-Fi* hotspots around their nation, internet is slow and frustrating for everybody. Firewood is gathered in communal areas enabling the crown virus to easily travel between the people collecting it.

Today's sun has yet to rise over a land of snow-topped sand and feelings of defeat. Walking alone in the predawn darkness with a downcast gaze is Emory. The cautious optimism of this short, sinewy elder has been depressed by current events. Snow crunches under the soles of her moccasins she sluggishly trudges through the icy roads. Cold intensifies as the northern wind blows snow off adobes and onto her small figure. Emory's teeth chatter as she shivers in the worsening weather. When the wind dies down, she faces the adobes with her eyelashes dusted with snow like a white mascara. The rising sun gilds the land with its yellow light. Snow accumulating on adobes beautifully glitters in the sun like diamonds.

The rising sun restores peace to Emory's mind. A smile stretches across her thin, tired face. She closes her eyes while deeply inhaling the invigorating cold air. Snow circles around Emory as if she were a figurine in a snow globe. After the sun rises, Emory goes home and prepares for the tribal government's virtual conference.

* * * * *

Weak sunlight continues to shine over the Hopi Nation, painting the landscape in shades of gold and blue. The sand on top of the mesas glitters like gold coins. Below, deep-blue shadows envelop traditional Hopi brown clay homes. Wrapped in one of these royal-blue shadows is Emory's humble adobe. Seated on a chair woven from fibrous plants, her feet barely touch the rug made from old rags and towels.

Emory turns her computer on. It rests over a small home office table made from intricately twisted grasses. Emory waits for the tribe's online meeting to begin. Today's topic is the damaging potential the crown virus disease possesses. She enjoys piki bread, made from blue cornmeal, with traditional greenthread tea boiled over an open fire. Just as Emory swallows the last swig of tea from a University of Arizona mug, the computer produces a multitude of *Ding!* noises. Everyone slowly joins the meeting.

The Hopi tribal president, Mr. Loloma, clears his throat and says, "Everyone should openly express their feelings about the current circumstances."

A Hopi elder spits, "Protesting quarantine? Who does that? What a luxury!" while slamming a tribal-patterned mug on her table. She continues disclosing her contempt by adding, "White people value money over people because they make other people work just so they can purchase frivolities despite the dangerous pandemic. We can't let our people die from another disease. We've lost too much land, resources, people, and our own culture already."

A calmer council member responds to the outrage by saying, "How White people live their lives is up to them. Yes, we have lost a lot. No, we do not deserve to lose more. But all we can do is stay true to our ways and hope for the best."

People are silent until the nation's treasurer, Sinquah, informs people, "Every business in our nation has filed for bankruptcy. Today's poverty is the worst in Hopi history. Our people want to protest quarantine because the money we need for survival is vanishing!"

Everyone in attendance quietly ponders the burden of insufficient funds to purchase basic necessities and becomes silent. Some have been wondering if quarantine would do more harm than good.

Before any conclusions are reached, the oldest woman in the virtual meeting reminds everyone, "We've been through this before. The Regime repeatedly steals from us. They took our food and water. They ransacked our homes. Separated our families. The only consistency they deliver to us is hardship. Landlords of the Regime would love for us to take to the streets, protesting quarantine, and then die of infection. But we can't let that happen! Civil unrest is the hallmark of Western civilization. We must stay true to our way of peace to survive."

Everyone seems aware of this truth. Yet the fear of hunger and cold from bankruptcy still lurks in the air.

People remain silent until Sinquah asks, "What do you suggest we do?"

Someone responds, "Our Navajo neighbors are suffering gravely. We could be next. The Navajo Nation has instilled the strictest curfew of the Regime. We should continue following their lead."

Sinquah is dissatisfied with that answer. She challenges, "How will quarantine reverse poverty? Yes, we lived without money until conquest. Yes, we've survived pandemics before. Yes, everyone can die. Quarantine won't calm people's fear of losing everything they've come to rely upon. Few remember the old ways. Most of what Hopis desire today requires money. If we can't secure funds, people will protest quarantine and endanger everyone's health. We might not want to accept this, but we need money to survive."

No one likes acknowledging the consequences of colonization. Time passes in angry silence.

The group's taciturnity was broken by the optimistic Emory, who claims, "We are an ancient people who have lived without money until recently. Quarantine can help us survive the crown virus. I've been communicating with Hopis who practice the old ways. I learned that people have stashes of medicinal plants. Some still harvest cotton for clothes and blankets. We even have our own Hopi farmers! So we don't need to protest anything. We have everything we need right here! Oh, and did you forget about the Blue Kachina sighting? We are in the end times. How we act is imperative for the people of this world. Winter solstice passed us last month, and you know what that means! The Kachinas left the San Francisco Mountains and are coming to visit us. When the Kachinas arrive, they can help us. But only if we do what is right. Therefore, we must quarantine and adhere to tradition."

Everyone is humbled by Emory's reminder. The Hopi know that they shouldn't succumb to the ways of colonizers. Yet the pandemic-related stress diminishes the perceived power of the Blue Kachina.

In his deep solemn voice, Louis Loloma asks, "What resources do we have?"

Before Emory could continue, someone picks up a wicker basket full of cotton and chimes, "Look here! Remember this plant? Our ancestors used it for weaving. Every year, I harvest this cotton to practice traditional weaving. Across the years, I have collected enough cotton so all Hopis can have blankets and warm clothes in case of an emergency. Perhaps we can make face masks and gloves from it too?"

A healer adds, "I regularly collect medicinal plants. Traditional medicines might not cure the crown virus. But it could ease the symptoms."

Other traditional healers inform the tribal council about their collections of natural medicines.

Naha, Kotutuwa's grandmother, reminds people, "My grandson has always been a successful farmer! I work with other women to grind and store the maize harvested in our nation. Together, we have amassed enough cornmeal to feed everybody."

Some women in attendance nod their heads to confirm possessing stashes of cornmeal.

Discovering these hidden resources eases the fear of dependency on money and dread of bankruptcy.

Mr. Loloma clears his throat and says, "I will write our current curfew recommendations into law like what our Navajo neighbors have done. To survive, we must quarantine. Let's encourage people to be grateful for the resources we have and to share them freely."

The meeting is adjourned on this positive note. New curfew laws are being enforced by tribal police. Council members post warnings that "*the virus does not move, people move it. If people stop moving the virus stops moving and dies.*"

* * * * *

News of the disclosed resources fills the relieved Hopi Nation with joy and hope. Elders instill gratitude by reminding younger generations, "Money is just an object. Something we have lived without until recently." Wide audiences eagerly learn Hopi crafts, which were endangered before the pandemic. Face masks, warm clothes, blankets, and gloves are being made from Hopi tapestries and shared freely. Traditional medicine is produced in large quantities and relieves the ailments of sick Hopis which takes pressure off of the underfunded tribal hospital.

Kotutuwa and other Hopi farmers plan extensive cultivation for spring. They brainstorm ways to achieve the highest crop yield. This year, crops from the Hopi Nation might be the resident's only source of food. But if farmed successfully, everyone will be fed!

The Hopi team up and utilize what they have in this unfair world. Resourcefulness might save the Hopi from annihilation. They have no control over the money donated to the Navajo Hopi COVID-19 Relief Fund, but at least the Hopi have control over themselves.

THE PANDEMIC AND
THE DINÈ PART 2

People all over the world are forcefully united by suffering from the same crown virus. Of all countries that have been victimized by the ensuing plague, the Regime has been hit hardest. In the Regime, the Navajo Nation, with a population 498,320 residents, is the most diseased, and Navajo residents have the highest fatality rate in the world. Bad behavior has followed the pandemic's outbreak because theft and civil unrest are at an all-time high.

Navajo elder and medicine man Jim Sweetwater recently gave a lecture about the consequences of bad behavior, which his grandson Redwing posted on YouTube. Those who watched the video have been incentivized to adhere to Dinè morality. Good behavior is further encouraged by tribal police, actively enforcing the new virus prevention laws. Increased policing has brought thieves to prosecution and victims of theft reunited with their "missing" belongings.

Pressure to quarantine also increases with the change of seasons. Temperatures have dropped, and snow blankets the crimson landscape in white. This chilly atmosphere is undesirable for anyone who ventures outside. Furthermore, gray clouds block the waning sun and blend over the reservation's unsightly wintery monochrome expanse.

This bleak scenery accurately portrays the growing defeat and loss of hope the Dinè feel against the aggressively expanding crown virus. Despite being held captive to a wealthy and medically advanced country, the population of sick and dying Dinè rises daily. The pandemic death toll is most evident at the Navajo Health Center.

The Navajo Health Center is the Navajo Nation's largest hospital. As is the case with most hospitals managed by the Indian Health Services, it lacks adequate funding, resources, and staff. In this pandemic, with the inadequacy of this hospital, Navajo residents are fed up with IHS's failures and are making this hardship known to those off the reservation by posting on social media. In response, a lot of sympathy but little real help has been received.

To cope, the Dinè are forced to make do with the little they have. Inadequately equipped buildings are transformed into maladaptive, makeshift hospitals. Lacking sufficient personal protective equipment, healthcare workers risk contracting the fatal infection by re-wearing their "war" gear. The crown virus entered the Navajo Nation only two months ago. Already, healthcare workers are getting sick from exposure and collapsing from exhaustion during their lengthier shifts. In this understaffed hospital, the fate of the sickly Dinè worsens.

Outside the Navajo Health Clinic's virus battleground, the tribal government passes legislation to quell the plague. The threatened reservation is confined by an intense self-imposed lockdown and fortification attempt. Until further notice, no one is allowed entry to the Navajo Nation. Residents are disallowed from leaving unless they have an exceptional reason approved by the tribal government.

Lockdown is an essential protection for the many Dinè whose health complications increase their vulnerability to the contagious disease. Remote, temporary living centers have been established for the isolative protection of the most at risk Dinè with diabetes and hypertension. Elders who are also highly susceptible to infection, are encouraged to relocate to the living centers to minimize their exposure. This new transition further distresses Dinè elders who have never lived separately from their extended family.

Tensions develop between the remaining family members after losing the daily guidance of grandparents. Most Dinè are unemployed and can't afford gas for their vehicles. Even if escaping the confines of their *Hogan* was affordable, tribal police aggressively ticket lockdown violators. Quarantine transforms the cozy one-roomed *Hogans* into irritating cages for entire families. Winter is traditionally a time for grandparents to entertain youngsters with funny stories and traditional teachings. This winter children have more time to pick fights. As a result, people begin resenting those they love—people whom they lived with peacefully before the pandemic.

Neighbors routinely worked together gathering firewood and medicinal plants before the social distancing paradigm. Now laws prohibit physical interaction between household and nonfamily members. Each winter the Navajo Nation gets about two feet of snow. This winter it feels deeper and harder to traverse and the miles separating *Hogans* make neighbors feel even more isolated, lonely, and forgotten. People feel oppressed by emptiness. Even if neighbors lived closer together, laws still prohibit them from being close to each other, forcing thousands of residents to ration fire kindling and food during the challenging winter.

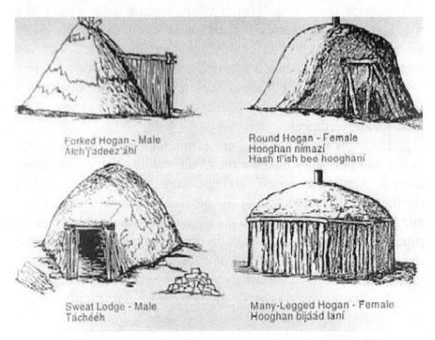

Forked Hogan - Male
Alch'adeez'áhí

Round Hogan - Female
Hooghan nimazí
Hash tl'ish bee hooghaní

Sweat Lodge - Male
Táchééh

Many-Legged Hogan - Female
Hooghan bijáád lání

Lockdown has also impacted people's reliance on the internet. Closed schools and stores force people to rely on Wi-Fi for their outside communication. But many homes lack electricity; therefore, Wi-Fi is frequently nonexistent.

Soaring tensions increase when Dinè children are unable to access their online classes. But education has become a lesser priority as infection threatens to obliterate entire families. In this adverse situation, many students accept defeat and that they will fall even more behind in school. Some will even be forced to forfeit graduation.

This consequence of quarantine worsens the already bad racial disparity of the Regime's scholastic achievement. Before the pandemic, Native Americans had the lowest high school graduation rate of all ethnicities in the Regime. Less than a third of indigenous students graduate from high school. Native Americans also hold the lowest college degree rate. While 28 percent of mainstream citizens hold bachelor degrees or higher, only 13 percent of natives do.

Education is vital to securing a high-paying job in the twenty-first century. The current disparity of education among Native Americans blocks them from accessing the opportunity, wealth, and status other ethnicities enjoy. This disparity in education combined with other factors contributes to the high rate of poverty on reservations.

* * * * *

Similar to all other elders, Jim Sweetwater is highly susceptible to contracting crown virus. Jim isolates himself with his teenage grandson Redwing at the base of the mountain with no name. Beyond safely isolating, Jim and Redwing want to heal the world through the Evil Way Ceremony. After the ceremony is completed, all land beneath the mountain's summit will become great again. Mountains in the Navajo Nation are named for their resources. The mountain Jim and Redwing have fled to has no name because it lacks resources. Consequently, this mountain is frequently ignored and deemed insignificant. Few people travel here, making it a safe place to quarantine.

A *Hogan* built in the old style from gray stones waits at the mountain's base. Despite having been abandoned centuries ago, it provides great shelter for Jim and Redwing. Outside cold wind whistling around the mountains swirl snow in spirals.

Inside, the duo sit beside a toasty fire, snacking on currants gathered and preserved by Jim's youngest daughter, Haseyah. A freshly hunted deer, collected during the trek, roasts over the fire and fills the *Hogan* with a savory aroma.

Streams and wildlife surround this place of safe isolation and durable shelter. After they complete the Evil Way Ceremony atop the mountain with no name, all land beyond this safe space will become great again. Before executing the ceremony, lengthy preparations and the completion of smaller ones must occur. But now, Jim and Joe are exhausted from trekking miles to this *Hogan*. After the deer has finished roasting, its meat will be dried and both men will rest for the night.

At the crack of dawn, Jim wakes his grandson by saying good morning in Dinè Bizaad: "*Ya'at'èè abini!*" In response, the still sleepy Redwing stretches and groans before the duo exit the *Hogan* to greet the day. Outside, they begin by dispersing yellow corn pollen while running from east to west in the traditionally symbolic direction their ancestors took to reach Dinetah. They then reenter the *Hogan*, put their long locks in the traditional Dinè bun, and eat breakfast. The duo's first project is building a sweat lodge for purification. After breakfast, the search for materials and construction begins. Jim has chosen to speak as little English as possible during this time of preparation and ceremony, so Redwing becomes fluent in Dinè Bizaad.

Today, after twelve long days of construction, the sweat lodge is complete. Jim and Redwing now have a place to purify themselves for the upcoming ceremonies.

Jim places his thickly-calloused hands on his wide hips while checking their work. After detailed scrutiny, he approves the project. Jim looks at his grandson, his lively coal-colored eyes beaming with pride, and says, "Well done, my dear. One day, you will be responsible for replicating this structure for your family and community."

Redwing smiles at his grandfather and asks, "Can we try it?"

Jim nods approval and hands a piece of flint and kindling to his grandson signaling for him to start the sauna.

After hours have passed, it is now dusk as the duo awake from their cleansing rest. Jim and Redwing yawn and stretching their limbs before exiting the sweat lodge.

They silently walk across the dark, rocky earth and wade in the cold, shallow stream to wash their sweat off. Shiny stars are reflected in the stream, appearing to dance in the current. Next, they return to eat roasted venison and dried yucca in the *Hogan*. While eating, Jim and Redwing happily reflect upon their progress thus far.

After supper, both men lie on sheepskins from livestock Jim's eldest daughter raised on the ranch and bequeathed from Jim's late wife, and they doze off.

Early the next day, Jim and Redwing begin the Blessing Way Ceremony which is the precursor to the Evil Way Ceremony. They responsibly rise before dawn to greet the new day, running from east to west while sprinkling yellow corn pollen. Gusts of cold wind collect the dispersed pollen into small, gold clouds before carrying it out of sight. After the pollen is carried away, the duo sings part of the Blessing Way prayer.

> Today as I walk out, today everything evil
> will leave me. I will be as I was before, I will
> have a cool breeze over my body. I will have
> a light body, I will be happy forever, nothing
> will hinder me. I walk with beauty before me.
> I walk with beauty behind me. I walk with
> beauty below me. I walk with beauty above me.
> I walk with beauty around me. My words will
> be beautiful. In beauty all day long may I walk.
> Through the returning seasons may I walk. On
> the trail marked by pollen may I walk. With dew
> about my feet may I walk. With beauty before
> me, may I walk. With beauty behind me, may I
> walk. With beauty below me, may I walk. With

beauty above me, may I walk. With beauty all
around me, may I walk. In old age wandering
on a trail of beauty, lively, may I walk. In old
age wandering on a trail of beauty, living again,
may I walk. My words will be beautiful.

By the time they finish singing, the sun is shining. Today is
unusually warm for winter, and some of the snow begins to fall off
boulders and trees. Small flowers pop out of the snow as though
they are making an optimistic appearance for the Ceremony. Soft
thuds of snow sliding off scraggly tree branches echo across the
land.

After eating breakfast and wrapping their long locks in the
traditional Dinè bun, Jim and Redwing paint themselves with
red and white clay. Elaborate sand paintings are drawn upon the
ground, encircling the glowing fire in the *Hogan's* middle. When
the circle of sand paintings is complete, Jim picks up an abalone
shell full of mugwort and sweetgrass then signals his grandson
to light it. Small sparks diffuse into smoke as the plants smolder.
Redwing then picks up his abalone shell bowl and lights the palo
santo and sweetgrass inside.

With Redwing following the footsteps of his grandfather,
the duo sings the "Song of Creation" while traversing the sand
paintings from east to west. After all the sand paintings have been
mixed together by the marches of Jim and Redwing, the men exit
the *Hogan* garbed in clay and traditional clothes. Good energy
wafts into the surrounding land as the Blessing Way prayer is
repeated eleven more times.

On the final rendition, the sun pierces the clouds, making
the white winter surroundings glow in the light. Smiles stretch
across the melancholy faces of Jim and Redwing as they feel a
sense of accomplishment for conducting the ceremony. But their
work is not quite done. Due to the severity of evil, the Blessing
Way Ceremony will need to be completed eleven more times with
a day of purification and collection of resources before the day of
the ceremony.

THE HOPI AND THE VIRUS PART 2

Winter is typically the most devastating period of the Regime's sick season. While the crown virus is still at large, the frigid high desert winter in the Hopi Nation has finally passed! Now gentle spring rain melts the remaining snow. Newly formed streams trickle down the mesas to water the crops below. Flowers of every color bloom throughout the desert sands while rainbows fill the expansive blue sky above. The flourishing wildflowers echo the revival of ancient ways. Hopis studied their cultural traditions for respite during the frosty captivity of winter. Tradition has afforded the people some salvation; however, its success is finite.

Since the colonizer's arrival centuries ago, the Hopi have yearned for them to return to Europe or in the very least respect Native Americans. While Europeans have yet to go home, this pandemic has distanced the two rivals. Despite the Hopi Nation's growing separation from colonizers, the reliance on European inventions remains. However, the usage of European inventions is now cumbersome. The mainstream society is hoarding the parts needed for European inventions to work, and the few available replacement parts are unattainable because Hopis are prohibited from leaving the reservation to buy them. Residents have become frustrated by their non-working products of Western civilization. This experience reveals that distance from colonization is not what the Hopis wished for. Spring is usually a happy time. This spring, few are happy because of these circumstances.

All Hopis are currently unemployed and now spend their days voluntarily enduring the monotonous physical labor of planting maize, melons, and squash. Under the leadership of Kotutuwa and other Hopi farmers, residents work to feed the tribe. But sustainable farming doesn't provide cash to pay the cable TV, electricity, and phone bills. This outcome irritates people when they return home from a hard day's work and are deprived of their favorite electronic entertainment.

Ancient Hopis enjoyed downtime and used it to acquire knowledge from their elders. In the twenty-first century, boredom and downtime are novelties because people are inundated with devices. Boredom has become such a novelty that confuses the colonized minds still dependent on persistent entertainment. Sometimes, the desires for instant gratification spark aversion to the old traditional ways.

Stuck in the daily monotonous rut, Hopis long for nighttime when they can search the heavens for the Red Kachina. A Red Kachina sighting will signify that this world is about to be purified. Shortly thereafter, the Red Kachina will relieve the Hopis from ongoing boredom.

Tonight, like the past nights, Hopis gather atop the mesas to gaze at the stars, each family compliantly sitting six feet away from the next. Expansive blackness envelopes everyone and everything in the veil of night, punctuated by tiny sparkles of ordinary stars.

Tonight's stars foretell that tomorrow will be just like today, yesterday, the day prior, and the day before that. Everyone feels trapped in these long excruciating days, a purgatory of existence. Soon, the star the Hopi are searching for will manifest itself, and relief from ongoing boredom and colonization will follow. Until the Red Kachina shines, people can only wait and live the same day over and over and over again.

As unfavorable as boredom is, it is a petty consequence of colonization. European societies claim that colonization "developed" indigenous lands and helped native peoples. But the opposite is true. Colonization has always been executed to benefit Europeans with few considerations made for the people native to the land under siege. Even crumbling infrastructure which are remnants of colonization favor the invaders over the Natives.

For example, the Hopi Nation is full of roads the tribal government can't afford to pave. Dilapidated and unwanted shacks built according to a European blueprint stand beside the dirt roads. Europeans built this infrastructure with the good intention of "developing" Hopi land. This construction sits on ancient farming plots and prevents Hopis from using the land in the best way. However, contrarily, Europeans who visit the Hopi Nation can easily follow the dirt roads the Hopi despise.

The third mesa, center of the universe is also referred to as the black mesa due to large coal deposits. A wealthy corporation made a massive profit by pilfering the sacred mesa for coal. The Hopi were paid a meager portion of the massive profit attained by the mining company's leaders and shareholders from exploiting Hopi land. The largest payment the Hopis received was the debilitating health of those who, for a minimum wage, retrieved coal for colonizers. Naha, who is a member of the American Indian Movement (AIM), led other Hopis to protest the mining company's questionable ethics. AIM relentlessly defended Hopi land for which they received mysterious threats. Naha agonizingly decided to stop fighting the mining company forty years ago when her daughter, Kotutuwa's mother, returned home from Hopi High School brutally beaten by unidentifiable White men that Naha believes to be from the mining company.

When the mesa ran out of coal, the wealthy corporation lost interest in further developing the Hopi Nation and abandoned it altogether. In addition to disregarding the Hopi's desire for economic development, the mining company left the hazardous waste from coal extraction, sickened workers, and desecrated land. Despite such abandonment, Naha still sporadically receives mysterious threats for her act of protest.

Other tribes have suffered similar unethical outcomes from ventures with businesses catering to colonizers. Despite the many cases of corporate cruelty, mainstream citizens remain ignorant of the damage their demands inflict upon the Indigenous. Regardless, the value Indigenous people place on conveniences from colonizers is the most upsetting aspect of colonization.

Cars ease travel across the Hopi Nation's 2,531 square miles of sand and mesas. But money, the currency of colonizers, is needed for cars to work. Money has recently vanished in the Hopi Nation, and cars are quickly running out of gas.

Life has always been strenuous for the Hopi to survive the harsh desert climate. Hardiness and extensive labor were required to cope with and endure living here. Yet the conveniences of colonization have altered everyone's idea of what hard work is. As a result, members wonder if returning to the normalcy of Hopi tradition is even plausible. As damning as the consequences of colonization are, a greater injustice remains. The biggest threat facing Native Americans is the negligence of White dictatorships.

For centuries, the Regime has promised an abundance of things Natives have yet to receive. Despite failing to fulfill promises made long ago, the Regime continuously forces Native Americans to pay taxes and allow regime corporations to exploit tribal lands. Companies created and run by colonizers are well versed in escaping retribution for any wrongdoing. The coal company mentioned earlier has yet to make amends for the harm afflicted upon the Hopi people. Instead of helping people by donating profits, wealthy companies demand that they are applauded for creating things manufactured to malfunction on stolen land.

When the crown virus began ascending to power, the Hopi tribal government hoped the remoteness of their nation would separate them from disease. While the crown virus has yet to ransack the Hopi Nation the way it has the Navajo Nation, Hopis are still getting sick. The world seems to have turned a blind eye to the plight of Native Americans since few have donated to the Navajo Hopi COVID-19 Relief Fund. The unfairness of being far removed from the world but close to plague haunts everyone.

At the dawn of disease, traditional practices successfully fulfilled the need for warm clothes and face masks. Unfortunately, the industriousness of the Hopi tradition has limits. Traditional remedies don't suffice for ventilators or emergency oxygen. In this pandemic, traditional medicines only delay death. This usurping of hope gravely disappointed everyone depressing Hopis who have routinely been let down before. Despite being committed to peace, the surviving Hopis emotionally share tension and rampant frustration of colonization.

Everyone in the Hopi Nation acknowledges that they are living in the final days of this world. Yet these past few months have been so boring and lacking in purpose that Hopis now beg the Red Kachina to destroy Earth. Even when the purification comes, another unknown remains. The Hopi Prophecy is unclear about what to expect in the fifth world. The prophecy does disclose, however, that it will have a unique challenge. So what will be endured next?

Hopefully, the struggles of the fifth world won't be so vexing as those of this current world. No one knows but everyone accepts the possibility that the fifth world might have similar struggles to this current world, with similar circumstances they will suffer through all over again. If such is the case, is it even worth staying true to traditions and passing the tests of this world to move forward?

Since the dawn of European invasion, the Hopi people have strived to go forward with their way of life regardless of persecution. But what if the reward for cultural survival isn't worth the struggle? Could their entire existence in an unfair world be a waste of time?

THE SNEEZE

Spring blossoms decorate trees and perfume Regime cities. Windblown flower petals decorate the sidewalks like pink snow. Mainstreams only think positively when walking beneath the sweetly scented blossoming trees and over mosaics of fallen petals. The sun further encourages people's optimism and longing to go outside by extending its yellow rays to warm and invigorate the earth.

All seems well in the lovely fresh spring. But the crown virus casts a shadow of doubt by resurging and continuously infecting people. Citizens get aggravated and exhausted by the daily virus prevention protocol despite the unrelenting disease. Spring's ephemeral beauty and warm weather spark embers of animosity among citizens who are continually instructed to isolate and stay indoors, thereby forfeiting nature's renaissance. Regime citizens have a tradition of throwing tantrums when denied what they want.

But only a few quarantine protestors remain. Last winter, thousands of people expressed their grievances about virus prevention protocols to exhausted healthcare workers and first responders. Acting in dumb defiance, most challengers succumbed to an illness they insisted to be a governmental hoax. The following months have been deadly silent with the demonstrators' passing.

Multitudes of early deaths infuriate those who constantly blame their problems on every imaginable scapegoat. But in a rare turn of events, these troublesome people have become the minority. The rising crown virus death rate has fostered unusual behavior. Instead of sparking a catalyst for complaint, people finally start to practice gratitude.

The pandemic has limited the supply of resources that were previously immediately available. Growing pains from not having immediate access to resources have led to the mainstream citizen's discovery that earth's treasures are finite. Today, most people accept that they can't have everything and rejoice over what they do have.

Furthermore, the shortage of on-demand things has forced citizens to understand the hurdles of the homeless. Inspired by this new experience, many citizens use their time in quarantine to plant crops for the transients.

The mainstream society is full of people metamorphizing into altruists. Yet one particular person is an exemplary example of the recent change.

John Doe lives in a cheap apartment stashed in an unmaintained apartment complex for the middle class. He appears much older than he really is due to his pre-pandemic sedentary lifestyle. In fact, if the crown virus hadn't risen to power, he may never have gotten off his couch.

His mother, who formerly lived in an assisted living center across the street, was among the first to die from the crown virus. Her death was exasperated by protestors who delayed the ambulance transporting her by blocking the hospital. At first, he was overcome by bitterness toward protestors. However, this loss forced him to see the price of human greed. It also sparked a desire to help others.

Today, after months of brooding, John is a changed man. Leading all residents in the apartment complex, John now oversees the largest neighborhood co-op vegetable garden. People who would have gone hungry have been fed from the crops grown from the garden John manages.

The pandemic has benefited vagabonds in other positive ways. As the Regime's silent majority, drifters are frequently neglected and resented by both the government and citizens who can afford housing. Yet homes once inhabited by quarantine protestors are now vacant from their death.

Vagabonds flock to empty homes for refuge. Consequently, those who can afford housing lose the privilege of distancing themselves from the destitute. As a result, citizens are hearing and empathizing with the vagabond's stories, a different perspective of the Regime. The shared stories encourage everyone to acknowledge the widespread poverty and oppression in the Land of the Free. This startling new reality has even the most devout of patriots beginning to question their loyalties.

Before the pandemic, mainstream citizens had a tradition of welcoming new neighbors with flowers. In this pandemic, people welcome unofficial residents with virus prevention products.

Each time those without shelter move into vacant homes and tell their neighbors of their hardship, faith in the Regime deteriorates. However, Regime police are unknowingly the biggest challengers of patriotism. Doing their civil duty, cops evict vagabonds from houses they didn't buy. Fortunately, constables recommend places where people without homes can legally reside. However, most "suggestions" are dead ends, forcing vagabonds back to the streets during an epidemic.

In times past, Regime citizens wouldn't have cared about anyone being evicted except for their own friends and family. Recently, they have come to understand and accept the impoverished as fellow humans and become irritated about their new neighbors being sent to the streets. Fairness is further questioned when police officers fail to enforce virus prevention protocols but will evict homeless people during a pandemic.

Constables might think they are edifying order by evicting intruders. Unbeknown to them, they are starting a rebellion. Across the Regime, shortchanged citizens unite in their threatened thoughts. *Something must be done to change this unfairness—to challenge this system from which few people benefit.*

Unanimously, the silent majority desire change. For they now know the Regime is not the Land of the Free. Tired of being mistreated and being the mainstream societies' scapegoat, angry vagabonds unite with hopes of a better world. Even those with resources feel lied to and shortchanged by the governors. To cope, citizens now pay attention to their surroundings. Their intention is to find a cause for which to usurp the Regime.

Regime citizens are becoming more cognizant of the world around them, and patriotism declines. Yet governors remain unaware of their captives' change of heart. Soon citizens will sneakily exile their landlords the way one purges irritants by sneezing.

THE PANDEMIC AND
THE DINÈ PART 3

The dark icy Navajo Nation winter has passed. Each day is warmer than the one before. Under a cloudless indigo sky, the sound of melting snow percolates through the red soil, replenishing the groundwater below. Flowers of every color blossom in budding maize fields and perfume the air with their sweet scent. Adding to these pleasantries, the Blessing Way Ceremony has been completed by Jim and Redwing. Their blessings created a reservation-wide sense of peace and confidence. With it, the Navajo Nation residents are joyful for the first time this calendar year.

Happy at last, no one wants to accept that their peace of mind seems irrational. Although fresh flowers, spring greenery, and warm weather are enjoyable, none of these are effective weapons against the crown virus pandemic. In the Navajo Nation, the past months have been marked by infection, turmoil, and grief. The Dinè hope for better days. But death and destitution from the pandemic continue.

Tribal police continue to relentlessly enforce the Regime's strictest virus prevention protocols. Yet the Navajo Nation still has the highest crown virus death rate in the world. Suffering the most are the Navajo Clinic health care workers. Exhausted medical staff can't rest because the clinic has been at capacity for months. Severely ill patients are airlifted to hospitals in neighboring states. Even with this help, resources are stretched beyond their capacity and few sick people recover.

Instead of focusing on their latest misfortune, the people resort to delusion. Resilient and steadfast Dinè continue to entertain unlikely hopes of a positive outcome. Yet some Dinè believe relief will never come and have accepted defeat.

Unbeknown to all, help is on the way. Upon arrival, the donated help will alter the fate of the Dinè.

A small island nation is separated from the Navajo Nation by half a continent and an entire ocean. The rocky gray shoreline of this island's beaches breaks and divides the cold, blue waves of the North Atlantic Ocean. Rain perpetually falls here, producing lush green fields. From abundant greenery, this island earned the name the Emerald Isle. Those who inhabit the Emerald Isle are culturally different from Native Americans. Yet both groups have endured similar fates of persecution.

During the 1800s, the Emerald Isle was invaded by a neighboring country called the Crown. With occupation, their food source was reduced to one staple crop, potatoes. When a viral blight spread through the island's potato crop, widespread famine, later named the Great Hunger, ensued. Untold numbers of agonizing deaths from starvation followed. Acting as a dictatorship, the Crown leveraged the famine-related deaths to expand their occupation of the Emerald Isle.

At the same time a world away, thousands of Dinè starved to death in the Bosque Redondo internment camp. After imprisoning Native Americans, the Regime which is the Crown's scion pilfered Dinè land. The brutal persecution endured by the Dinè facilitated empathy with the plight of the Emerald Isle natives. Filled with compassion, the Dinè selflessly gathered from their meager supply of clothes and food donations for far off people they would never meet. This act of charity resulted in an unlikely bond with the distant islanders.

Despite time and distance, the bond between the Dinè and the Emerald Isle remains strong. Today, both groups are unified by ongoing strife. The dictatorships that starved and stole land from the Dinè and the Emerald Isle still reign over them. Both peoples have had to fight ardently for cultural survival, but the entirety of their ancestral lands has yet to be returned.

Wanting to honor this unlikely friendship, a public monument memorializing the benevolence of Native Americans was erected near the Emerald Isle's capitol. This monument inspires Emerald Isle inhabitants to repay the Dinè for past generosity. Currently, the pandemic creates the opportunity to do that.

Collectively, the Emerald Isle government and citizens donate to the Navajo Hopi COVID-19 Relief Fund. By the time the crown virus is defeated, donations from the Emerald Isle will have accounted for most of the charity received.

Through their unlikely friendship, the Dinè and Emerald Isle reached out to and supported one another. In a world segregated by prejudice, borders, nationalities, citizenships, races, and religions, these two vastly different groups of people help each other in difficult times. Perhaps this proves that despite profoundly different beliefs and circumstances, we are all just humans with the same needs. If the radically different and geographically isolated Dinè and Emerald Isle inhabitants forged a lasting friendship, we all can.

Long live Ireland—the Emerald Isle of kind people!

* * * * *

Tomorrow the Navajo Nation residents will rejoice over the pleasant surprise of generous donations from the Emerald Isle. Tonight, while most people slumber, Jim and Redwing Sweetwater are wide awake outside the *Hogan*, preparing for the Evil Way Ceremony.

The dark night is illuminated by the distant glow of a pale full moon. Faint moonlight reaches only to the treetops as long shadows cast by the towering ancient trees obscure the ground below. The peculiar moonlight produces an eerie sense of a floating forest.

Lurking in the mountain's shadow, a yellow fire roars with life. Its flames challenge the power of expansive darkness. Thick blue smoke of sage and sweetgrass fill the dark air. The somber faces of Jim and Redwing are illuminated by the powerful flames. Both traditional Dinè are half-naked and their bodies glisten with sweat.

Each person rubs the fire's scented smoke over his head to purify thoughts. A wooden pipe filled with peyote and tobacco lays at their feet. Redwing isn't mature enough to smoke the pipe yet. So Jim has already taken three puffs over fifteen-minute intervals. Ready for the final puff, Jim bends at the hips and grasps his pipe. Pipe in hand, Jim stands perfectly straight purposefully inhaling and exhaling the cold night air before taking a final hot puff. While inhaling peyote, Jim closes his dull and distant dark eyes. Thick, potent smoke fills Jim's lungs as he turns his body toward the mountain with no name. Pungent gray smoke envelopes Jim as he exhales.

In Dinè Bizaad, the Navajo language, Jim announces that the Evil Way Ceremony will be conducted at the mountain's summit. Thunderclaps boom as Jim informs the Holy People about the thievery, disease, and other evils that have spread throughout the Navajo Nation. Only Jim can see the black lightning on this dark night. Silence follows Jim's completed explanation for why the Evil Way Ceremony must happen.

Suddenly a flash illuminates the land in an electric-blue color before everything becomes black again. Following this flash of blue lightning, bundles of sage topped with eagle plumes are extended toward the mountain with no name. Thick, translucent fog rolls in obscuring the summit while surrounding Jim and Redwing. Jim smiles when he sees sparks of red lightning flash above the clouds a show of nature's rare fireworks. Quick flashes of yellow lightning follow, making the surroundings glow. During these flashes, the men see the apex and clouds which are spiraled and look like Chindi.

The Holy People have been informed about where, when, and why the Evil Way Ceremony will take place. All preparations have been completed so the ceremony can be conducted. Cool refreshing rain now falls on the men below. Their fire is quickly extinguished. Before Jim and Redwing's eyes adjust to the enveloping darkness, a white comet circles the crown of the mountain. Rain has reduced logs from the fire to damp charred remains. On this crucial black night, the diffused, dim moon remains their only source of light.

THE PANDEMIC AND
THE DINÈ PART 4

Sufficient donations have mercifully arrived in the Navajo Nation courtesy of Emerald Isle citizens. Hope has accompanied this delivery as Dinè now believe they will be able to save themselves from the disease.

Adding to their optimism is the quickly approaching summer which usually signals the end of the Regime's sick season. That is when most of the Navajo Nation's economy-dependent tourism occurs. Outside the Navajo Nation's boundaries, crown virus death rates have decreased, allowing smaller Regime governments to ease their own virus prevention protocols.

The Navajo Nation has kept a strict lockdown during the pandemic. During these past long months, the Navajo Nation has been forced to sacrifice their frail economy, which profits from the whims of tourists, to keep the people safe. The absence of regular tourism has shattered the nation's fragile economy. Possibilities of reopening the Navajo Nation in time for the year's greatest influx of tourists are heavily debated.

Those in favor of tourism highlight the victories in the fight against the plague. Today, for the first time in months no new crown virus cases have been recorded in the Navajo Nation. This past week has been the first of the year not to be marked by a crown virus death. However, everyone keeps their optimism tempered by the great unknown future. Elders sense that despite this change of events, the worst is yet to come.

*****

The early summer night enshrouds Jim and Redwing Sweetwater in shadows as they ascend the scraggly mountain with no name. Tonight's moon is also hiding behind the scraggly mountain, so the climbers see nothing but darkness, adding challenges to their precarious journey. Hikers haven't traversed this trail the duo now climb since the pandemic started. Overgrowth increases the ardor Jim and Redwing must exert in creating a new path. In this dark land of crags and jumbled rocks, hands are used in place of eyes. With each movement, loose stones are dislodged and tumble to the base. Their ruckus creates the only noise apart from light rain. Clouds cling to the mountain and dampen its rocky cliffs. At the high altitude, water on rocks freezes over making them dangerously slick. Any mistake in climbing will cost Jim and Redwing their lives. Despite the risks, their ascension continues to help the sick and preserve this very tradition.

Air at the climbers' current altitude is thin and harshly frigid. Inhaling it stings the duo's airways like needles. Upon exhalation, small clouds are created and blend with those circling the mountain. Through this trek, Jim and his grandson become deeply connected with the shrouded mountain. For hours now, it is all they have contact with despite never seeing it. Redwing cautiously travels in the directly behind his grandpa, never letting Jim get beyond arms reach. Under the influence of peyote, Jim sees beyond the darkness. Light flickers at the summit signaling where to go. It appears someone is up there and expecting them.

Exhaustion from the taxing climb and increasing altitude results in seeing ordinary clouds transform into Chindi. Under the influence of peyote, Jim is particularly susceptible to this false pattern recognition. To him, apparitions of Chindi resemble stretched spiral bodies with blurred features. Each Chindi gives off unique and personal auras. Among them, Jim feels the presence of his dear wife, parents, friends, and other relatives who have crossed over. Encouragement from Ke'e visiting the physical world incentivizes Jim to continue onward despite the difficulty.

Chindi start to diminish as red and violet dawn streak across the sky. After climbing all night, both Jim and Redwing squint in the emerging light. Both men have been silent the entire climb. The lengthy, somber silence is broken by a sudden *"Ahèèhee'."* Redwing is puzzled by his grandfather's sudden announcement and looks up. In doing so, Redwing sees his grandfather standing upright on the summit of the mountain, smiling down at him. Jim extends a calloused hand and helps Redwing up to the apex. On the top of the world, Redwing happily announces "Ahèèhee'" to thank the Holy People for guiding them to the mountain's crown.

JUNE 19

Up to this point, the book's objective has been to highlight the horrific mistreatment the Regime has inflicted upon the Hopi and Navajo people. Yet the Regime's record would be incomplete without including its appalling abuse toward African Americans. For as different as Native Americans and Africans appear, their harrowing histories intersect in unfortunate ways.

The legacy of both peoples' maltreatment began in 1493. Back then, European greed exploded because Columbus returned home with gifts from Native Americans. Compelled by avarice, corrupt people abandoned their homeland to exploit the new world's unsolicited wealth.

European traditions of selfishness further egged on the conquistador's avarice because Western civilization is marked by conquest and caste. Foreigners who longed to ascend the slippery, unfair European institution of power and privilege never thanked indigenous hosts for gifting them resources. Instead, they always demanded more. Zeal for maximizing profits led the enterprises to use abusive free-labor practices. Native Americans became the foreigner's first slaves despite the fact that the colonizers were on indigenous land.

This enslavement was short-lived because millions of Native Americans died from old-world diseases, thereby limiting the colonizer's free labor. This unanticipated death by disease threatened to limit the profits of colonial enterprises.

On the other side of the world, tribal warfare was exploding across Africa. Strategically, warring tribes would abduct people from bands of enemies, thereby weakening rivals. Colonizers exploited the division within the African continent by purchasing prisoners of tribal warfare as slaves for the new world. In fact, people from Africa were more profitable slaves than Native Americans due to their experience in farming old-world crops and mining. Furthermore, the people of Africa were already immune to the old-world diseases, which nearly annihilated Native American slaves. Without consequence, the Regime ordered the capture and transport of Africans to the Americas, and they would be forced to labor without compensation from their new "owners." Now considered nothing but property, millions of enslaved Africans and their children would never be allowed to return home. Unfortunately, slavery has been practiced around the world for centuries. But Regime slavery was different. While most forms of slavery acknowledged slaves as humans with limited rights, the chattel slavery legalized in the Regime insisted that African slaves were nothing but European property. The initial US Constitution ratified this flawed logic with the three-fifths compromise, which directly states that each person from Africa is worth three-fifths of a white man. Multiple court cases have upheld Regime legality insisting that enslaved people are nothing more than tangible property which can be bartered.

Fortunately, mainstream citizens developed a conscience over time. Slavery changed during the Industrial Revolution. Machines with enhanced accuracy mass-produced free textiles, thereby limiting the need for free human labor. Widespread implementation of machinery, which worked long hours without fatiguing, encouraged citizens to ponder the ethics of slavery. But the Regime's Southern territory was unimpacted by the Industrial Revolution because that region profited from selling their cotton, which was picked by slaves, to textile mills in the Northern territory. When the North attempted to put limitations on the South's use of chattel slavery, plantation owners, whose raw materials supplied textile mills, decided to leave the country entirely and create their own nation under which chattel slavery would continue as they saw fit. The Regime president didn't want to lose money from the South's cash crops. As a result, four bloody years of civil war commenced. In the end, the North won and passed the Thirteenth Amendment, which declared slavery illegal on June 19, 1865.

Although the Regime changed its laws regarding slavery, the Regime has done little to actually help those who have been impacted by it. Worst of all, the legal practice of chattel slavery fostered an institution of racism from which Africans still suffer.

Today, the Regime is the wealthiest country in the world. Its wealth is the result of centuries of slave labor. Yet descendants of slavery have yet to be compensated for what their ancestors endured. Refusal to gift reparations to survivors of slavery is a prime example of the Regime's refusal to improve its injustice or do the right thing.

Another example is how police forces have historically operated. Regime police departments were established before the Thirteenth Amendment. Back then, the Fugitive Slave Act demanded that police officers catch and return runaway slaves to their "owners." To effectively uphold this responsibility, Regime police profiled roaming African citizens as escaping slaves. When the Thirteenth Amendment made slavery illegal, cops stopped targeting Africans as runaway slaves. However, Regime police were then responsible for enforcing new oppressive laws that segregated Africans from the rest of the mainstream society. Upholding those restrictive laws resulted in more continuous racial profiling. Eventually, the segregation laws against African Americans have been revoked. Today, people of all races can become a police officer in the Regime. However, many Regime constables still profile people from Africa. Modern racial profiling is most evidenced in the criminal justice system. Despite forming a racial minority in the large Regime population, African Americans have the highest incarceration rate in the world. They are also most likely to be pulled over by traffic cops and murdered under questionable circumstances by Regime police out of all other ethnicities today. Not all police officers are racist. In fact, many people from Africa work as constables. However, Regime policing started before slavery was outlawed.

So this unfortunate history is not a reflection of all police officers. If anything, it only shows how slowly the Regime has been to change for the safety and well-being of all citizens. Every day, constables do benevolent deeds, making the twisted history between police departments and racism an unfair stigma to all cops who died in the line of duty. In most mainstream cities, police officers are usually the first to arrive on scene at car accidents or other atrocities. They start CPR and provide first aid care before emergency medical services arrive. These quick actions in dangerous and stressful circumstances save thousands of civilian lives each year.

Beyond tragic accidents, law enforcement officers stop evil people from doing evil things every day. In doing so, law enforcement officers are frequently killed in the line of duty. It is tragic when they are murdered by civilians. Killing constables is immoral and unethical. It could also be offensive to label all police as racist and turn a blind eye to the good they do.

That said, even the noblest police officers fall prey to the Regime's racist classical conditioning. This is manifested in the overpolicing of neighborhoods with large percentages of African people. Changing the current system of racism should keep racial minorities safer than they currently are while also reducing the negative stigmas surrounding the police force.

The world might become a better place if citizens everywhere learned their country's true history, specifically when we discover what the governing landlords never want us to see. Hopefully, this knowledge will grant us the mental fortitude to hold entire governments, police forces, and militaries accountable for their malevolence. That said, it might be best if everyone treated fellow humans decently regardless of race, occupation, or citizenship. Today might be a good day to ponder the aforementioned facts because it is June 19, 2020—emancipation day! Unfortunately, African communities in the Regime have been pilfered by the pandemic and have the second highest crown virus death toll. Frail survivors host an online celebration for emancipation and draft plans for combatting twenty-first-century racism.

Ironically, June 19 isn't a federal holiday but Columbus Day is. Perhaps the perceived validity of these holidays further clarifies the Regime's priorities. But the crown virus has killed many bad people in the land. As an unforeseen side effect of the pandemic, Regime citizens become more concerned about the welfare of racial minorities. Today, more people outside the African community celebrate June 19 than ever before.

But the current forty-fifth president is among those who won't celebrate people being freed from slavery. Instead, he is hosting a party to celebrate his awesomeness! All guests have been permitted to defy virus prevention protocols in his white castle.

This landlord is under scrutiny for his negligent concern for African American rights and the crown virus. Tonight, his irresponsible behavior adds fuel to the fire raging against his reputation. Unlike this latest landlord, pandemic-related boredom has influenced Regime citizens eagerly listen to the African community. Those who are truly open-minded leave the June 19 celebrations with a new worldview. Slowly but surely, all people become enraged over how the Regime mistreats racial minorities.

Yet the president draws attention to himself in the closed confines of his white castle. Fearlessly, Europeans continue celebrating their perceived superiority while racial minorities brace for annihilation. To an outsider, the Europeans have indisputably won Native American land forever. But Newton proved that for every action, there is an opposite but equal reaction. Therefore, a day will come when the same quantity of blood the Regime drained from Africans and Native Americans will be drained from the evil Europeans dominating the Regime.

FINISHING THE EVIL
WAY CEREMONY

At the summit of the mountain with no name, Jim and Redwing Sweetwater view the surrounding world from the perspective of the Holy People. They see the surrounding environment sprawled out from distant snowcapped mountains feeding the rippling blue streams that wind down through green conifers.

Tears of joy slide down Jim's round cheeks as he faces his grandson and says, "Well done, my dear. You have learned much. It is now your responsibility to remember this ceremony for when it is needed again."

Redwing solemnly nods without shifting his gaze from the breathtaking view of the world below while positively reflecting on his daunting teamwork for the ceremony and the fact that the Dinè still exist in the Regime dictatorship.

Fog slowly evaporates from the sun as if the Chindi are off to slumber. This early morning sun has a powerful, ethereal energy to it. Under its radiant dawning light, mountains composed of regular rock appear to be made of obsidian. The forest below appears to form an emerald carpet parted by sapphire streams. At the summit of this splendor, the climber's skin glows in the sun like freshly minted copper coins. Jim's hair, streaked gray with age, shines like a multitude of silver chains. Joe's dark hair is the color of rich ebony.

After embracing the view, tiny circles of yellow corn pollen are ritualistically scattered from east to west from the summit into the valley below with blessings. The two steadfast Dinè sense that the Holy People are among them and are choosing to accompany them in today's Evil Way Ceremony. Sweetgrass is lit at Jim and

Redwing's feet in an abalone shell. They rub its cleansing smoke over their heads. Next, the smoldering sweetgrass is left to fill the air with its rich, earthy aroma. Prayers of ridding evil and healing all who have been afflicted by evil are chanted. As they finish the Ceremony, bundles of sage are removed from their coat pockets and held at arm's length while prayer to remove all evil from the earth is offered to the Holy People.

First, sage is pressed against foreheads to cleanse thoughts. Next, it is pressed against the mouth to cleanse evil words. Then it is held over the heart to cleanse emotions. Finally, the sage bundle is pressed against the solar plexus to cleanse the soul. This process is repeated three more times because Navajo metrics are based on the number four. After the fourth repetition, sage bundles are lifted to the mouths while inhaling. Sharply, they exhale while casting pale-green bundles into the smoldering fire.

A sense of peace usually follows the completion of the Evil Way Ceremony. Today, a peculiar, unsatisfied feeling lingers. Both men look at each other, trying to determine what went wrong. Something doesn't feel right. Yet the Evil Way Ceremony was executed correctly.

Desperate for answers, the summit is explored for a sign of acceptance from the Holy People. All that is found is an abandoned fire pit full of charred firewood. This pit appears to have been used by a climber before the pandemic.

"Weird," Redwing says while looking up to his grandfather for answers.

Jim walks to the edge of a cliff and furrows his bushy brows while gazing into the landscape below. After a moment of silence, Jim sighs and shrugs his shoulders like Redwing, and wraps one of his thick, strong arms around his grandson.

Jim leads Redwing down the mountain. Before descending the summit, Jim cautiously looks over his shoulder to make sure they're not being followed. No one is seen stalking the duo, yet Jim feels the unpleasantry of being watched. Together they leave the mountain, perplexed by troubling thoughts of why the Evil Way Ceremony didn't result in peace as they worry for the future.

Redwing, who is anxious to learn what this outcome means, struggles to patiently wait for an explanation. Jim only offers silence. On the listless trek down, every plant and rock passed is blessed to prepare for what's coming.

When the base of the mountain is reached, Jim assertively cups Redwing's round shoulders in his thick hands and sadly gazes into his dark eyes. Jim sighs and sternly says, "I don't know what to expect now. But I know that more is to come. We did all we could to help people. But something is furious, and our ceremony couldn't calm its rage. What happens next is beyond our control."

The grandson worriedly frowns and nods.

They arrive back at the *Hogan* where the duo resided for the ceremony. After packing their belongings, they give one last look at the mountain's summit. As the men look up, a figure quickly hides behind a boulder. But this sighting, if it is a sighting, happened too fast for either person to register it.

Together, the duo eagerly leaves the mountain with no name. Few words are spoken during the fifteen-hour hike home. Each person is in deep thought, fearing what's next but hoping for the best.

THE RED KACHINA

It is high noon on the eve of the summer solstice, but the unusually rainy weather across the Regime feels more like winter. Clouds and cold air have replaced the typically sunny and clear-blue June sky. Roads are obscured by the unseasonal downpour. Pedestrians slip and fall on the slick walkways. Of all Regime territories, the biggest falls are in a region called the Rust Belt. This is a down-trodden area of abandoned factories and broken promises of brighter futures. While most citizens in the Regime are impoverished, those in the Rust Belt are particularly penurious.

Adapting to this sudden change of weather, people quickly throw jackets on over their summer tops. They are also more willing to wear face masks than they have been all month. Only instead of wearing face masks to magnanimously curb the spread of the plague, people wear them to shield their faces from the strangely inclement weather.

Entering one of the many waterlogged streets is a teenager named Beatrice, fondly nicknamed Bea. Bea, with a naturally contagious smile, has many friends at school. But despite her humor and her happy-go-lucky outlook, she has surmounted many struggles.

Bea has lived her whole life in the rust belt and attends an underfunded and understaffed high school for disadvantaged youth. Beyond school, her only education comes from Regime-approved unreality TV.

At home, Bea's single mother of four children frequently works extra nursing shifts just to survive financially. Life would be easier if Bea's father paid child support, but he never does. As such, this family is left to fend for themselves with monthly fears of rationing food and eviction from the shabby apartment they call home.

Monetary security worries Bea as she walks to the grocery store. Bea's curly hair is woven into many small braids and set in a loose bun on top of her head, which sits beneath a big black umbrella. Her cheap plastic boots create ripples in the sloshing puddles. She wears a colorful face mask with pop stars on it, which she has consistently worn in public despite peer pressure not to.

Although she has yet to reach the legal age of adulthood set by the Regime, she is mature beyond her years. Despite being robbed of a proper education, Beatrice understands the reasons for virus prevention protocols. Reasons many Regime adults who have been to college can't or won't comprehend.

Bea knows the virus is dangerous because the local hospital is filled to capacity and makeshift hospitals are being forged in pandemically abandoned schools and gyms. Beyond these banal facts that many adults don't understand exists another reason for Bea knowing that the virus is real—her mother.

While working as a nurse on the pandemic hospital's front line, Bea's mother contracted the constrictive crown virus. Being the oldest of four kids, Bea must run the house until, and hopefully not if, her mother recovers. Mask haters are lucky not to physically suffer as Bea's mother currently is, or the way Bea's family is financially suffering without their single mother being up and able to work and bring home a paycheck.

Today, Bea is hesitant to go grocery shopping. Meager funds have become scarcer since her mother got sick with the crown virus and lost employment. The past few days, Bea has skipped meals to give more food to her siblings. She fears what will happen if the remaining money isn't enough for an adequate food supply. But today, Bea was forced to face this fear when she awoke to empty cupboards and hungry siblings.

Tonight, after grocery shopping, everything will change for Bea. She will bear witness to something horrible that will alter her life and most of the world. Presently, Bea is so wound up with worries of affording food that she is unable to think about the next hour, let alone tonight. When the sun goes down, Bea will be the catalyst for a much-needed change.

*****

Hundreds of miles away from the Rust Belt in the Hopi Nation, dark, swollen clouds block the sun. Today contrasts with the persistent swelteringly hot desert weather, which has dominated the past couple of months. These clouds are so thick and gloomy that people are driving with headlights on despite it being daytime. The heaviness of these clouds weighs down on the villages below, gradually dampening them with cool, misty fog. This type of weather is unusual for June in the desert. But at dusk, the clouds ominously divide as if an invisible hand is opening stage curtains. Shortly thereafter, the sun disappears behind the San Francisco mountains and darkness shrouds the land.

Below the third mesa, Kotutuwa and Hopi volunteers have completed harvesting his crops for the day. They know that growing and donating food is imperative since the crown virus has devastated the Hopi Nation economy. If the Hopi Nation farmers weren't supplying food, many villagers would have already starved to death.

After quickly packing the fresh maize, Kotutuwa gratefully dismisses the farm volunteers, who are startled by the sudden clearing of the sky, before he delivers the food to feed the hungry villagers of Oraibi. Old Oraibi has been recognized as the oldest continuously occupied town in the American continents. It's currently threatened with extinction by the twin threats of plague and poverty. While starting his truck, Kotutuwa ponders these threats facing his hometown and the strange damp weather and ominous clouds today.

Clouds provide optimism to the Hopis who rely on rain for all their water. However, this unexpected precipitation arouses suspicion. Right now, Kotutuwa fears that more strange and unusual things will occur when he least expects.

After his truck's engine roars with life, Kotutuwa nervously glances at the gas gauge of his dusty old maroon 1980s pickup truck. Months have passed since most of the Hopis received any income, so money for gasoline has become a luxury. Bouncing along the stony, potholed road, Kotutuwa prays that he has enough gas to travel from his farm to Oribi and back. The steeper the road becomes, the darker the sky gets. Kotutuwa feels that if it weren't for the trillions of small stars marking the night sky, he would be driving in a dark, limitless expanse of space. The steep road begins to plateau, and the tops of traditionally flat roofs are seen ahead. Kotutuwa is grateful that his truck has gotten him this far but rejoices too soon.

Hearing a sharp hiss, Kotutuwa's truck becomes difficult to control and one of the truck tires gets stuck in a pile of loose gravel. Kotutuwa wearily jumps out of his truck, armed with a flashlight, and slams the metal door behind him. Kotutuwa shines the pale-yellow circle of light onto the threadbare tires of his truck. A nail penetrating a worn tire causes anger to flash across his usually tranquil face. Exasperated, Kotutuwa kicks the side of his truck with his buckskin moccasin and curses the luck that appears to continually oppress the Hopi people.

*****

A man of African descent named Dale McHidal just finished his shift at work and walks down a street in the Rust Belt. Darkness quickly envelops the city as he walks away from his office. Despite being an essential worker, he never earns enough money for survival. Like many in quarantine, even among those whose work is deemed essential in this pandemic, his pay and hours of work hours are now reduced. But instead of complaining about his unfair financial situation, this resourceful employee uses what he earns to provide a better life for his daughters.

To save money, Dale has started commuting to work on his bike. Biking enables this man time to clear his head and get exercise since all gyms are closed. But today, his shift ends later than usual, and unbeknown to him, his life will end too. Dale whistles while walking to the bike rack where he locked his vehicle earlier today. Meticulously, Dale always puts his bike lock key in the right pocket of his jacket. Daunted by this morning's rain, Dale prioritized quickly escaping the elements for his office. While rushing, he forgot to correctly pocket the key. One can only imagine the gut-wrenching worry that befell Dale when the key was not felt in its usual place. Skeptically, he conducts a thorough search of all his pockets. A frail paper clip is all to be discovered tonight.

Dale holds the paper clip and ponders a way to open his bike lock without the key. Full of hope, he takes it out of his pocket and carefully wedges it into the bike lock. His hopes rise as he begins turning the paper clip. Anticipation of the lock opening and quickly returning home safely builds with every click. Suddenly the paper clip snaps in half inside the lock.

Distressed by the failure of his makeshift fix, Dale tries to remove the broken paper clip from the lock so he can begin again. The stubborn paper clip refuses to move, and Dale begins yanking on it with full force. When he is unable to remove the paper clip or open his bike lock, fury envelops him like sudden heat released from an opened oven on a cold day. He becomes charged with rage and angrily hurls the bike about. The bike lock is yanked as hard as possible away from the bike tire. But all attempts of freeing the bike fail. Suddenly a small circle of bright light falls on him, accompanied by the loud command, "Don't move!"

* * * * *

Fortunately, Beatrice was able to pay her much-needed groceries and relaxes while leaving the store. In this time of epidemic and economic trouble, small victories have a large impact. After a stressful day, she sees the rain has stopped pouring and the sky has cleared. In the darkness of night, Bea carries her groceries home.

Suddenly a streetlight turns on, revealing a path she never noticed before. Above, stars shoot over this trail as if to beckon her. A chill overcomes Bea as she ventures down this narrow trail. It leads her away from the glow of streetlights so that the stars are seen more clearly since the rain cleared smog from the sky. The path tightly weaves between jumbles of brambles and barbed wire. However, Bea ignores these obstacles and concentrates on the guiding stars above.

*****

Naha, the charitable grandmother of Kotutuwa, has graciously been distributing her grandson's crop donations to the Hopi villagers. Tonight, Kotutuwa is scheduled to deliver more crops. To pass the time waiting, Naham her traditional adobe home nestled into a Puebloan-apartment-like structure with a bundle of long grasses. After sweeping all dirt outside her yellow clay dwelling, Naha puts on a protective face mask she cut from traditional cloth and exits. A few paces away from her neighbor's adobes, Naha shakes the dust off of her broom.

Naha likes to wait for Kotutuwa on the steps leading up to her home so that they can catch up while social distancing. But tonight is so chilly that she reenters her adobe to retrieve a shawl. A sudden cold breeze prompts Naha to quickly pull her green-and-white–patterned shawl over her two gray braids. She continues to entirely wrap it around herself before sitting on the large stone steps. Her brown maple-syrup-colored eyes scan the dark horizon, anxiously searching for her grandson's headlights signaling his arrival. In the Regime, many racial minorities never make it home. She desperately hopes Kotutuwa won't become the next victim of a tragedy with questionable causes.

*****

Startled, Dale looks up but fails to see the face beyond the blinding white of the light.

Another sharp command from behind the light instructs, "Police! Put your hands where I can see them!"

Enraged and defiant, Dale yells back, "I can't get my bike!" while reaching for the bike lock.

The officer again shouts, "Police! Stand up and put your hands where I can see them!"

In return, Dale angrily says, "This is my bike, and I need to get home."

Still hiding behind the bright light, the officer yells, "This is your last and final warning. Stand up and put your hands behind your back!"

Feeling defeated and hoping for the best outcome, Dale gets up and grudgingly complies.

When Dale stands up and the officer sees no weapons, he commands, "Turn around and face me!"

Once again, Dale complies. When he turns around, Dale finally sees this unseen person of authority clearly. It is indeed a police officer. The officer continues bellowing commands that aren't followed. When the police officer pulls out handcuffs, Dale has had enough.

"I've had it with you!" he screams as he stands up and pushes the police officer away.

The police officer topples backward. Panicked, Dale decides to abandon his locked bike and run for his life. When the police officer gets up, he charges after the fleeing suspect. Just as Dale reaches the end of an ominously narrow trail bordered by brambles and barbed wire, the police officer aggressively tackles him as if preventing a touchdown in a football game.

* * * * *

Another glowing streetlight summons Bea at the end of the trail. Shortly thereafter, a strange visceral sensation encompasses her. Bea instinctively proceeds slowly and quietly. She suddenly clamps her hand over her mouth to muffle a shriek of horror over what she sees. Bea nervously swallows while chills of fear run down her spine like a million tiny spiders. The hair on the back of her neck stands up like that of a spooked cat.

As reason clears Bea's mind like cold water on a tired face, she ducks behind a twisted mass of brambles and takes out her phone. Thorny vines extend like multiple hands grasping for nonexistent help. Through the thorns, there is an opening just large enough for Bea to record on her phone the horror happening on the other side.

*****

Kotutuwa's foot achingly throbs from foolishly kicking his truck. He bends at the hips to catch his breath after a tirade of cursing. Feelings of defeat and anguish consume the exhausted farmer before he remembers that the Blue Kachina is voyaging to earth. Months ago, the Blue Kachina had broadcast itself as a star to signal the beginning of the end of this current world. Therefore, it is imperative to live each moment pure in heart regardless of obstacles.

After refocusing his thoughts, Kotutuwa blushes with embarrassment at his behavior and apologizes for it to the surrounding earth.

Calming down, Kotutuwa realizes that he can still get his crops to Oraibi with added effort. Besides, giving up is not an option when families will go hungry without his produce.

Resiliently, Kotutuwa scrapes rocks away from his truck's flattened tire. Kotutuwa shifts the gears into neutral and, with great effort, pushes his loaded truck onto the third mesa. Waiting villagers hear the approaching vehicle and eagerly come outside their homes in greeting. When Kotutuwa sees them, he dutifully puts his mask on his sweaty face and tiredly yells, "Flat tire! I need help!"

Donned in masks and protective gloves, villagers gladly rush over to help push with Kotutuwa's truck. Together, they get the truck to the middle of Oraibi. Usually, Kotutuwa drives his crops to his grandmother's residence where Naha and other elders distribute the harvest yields from Hopi farmers to hungry families. Tonight is different due to the flat tire. Villagers gratefully collect the food they need directly from Kotutuwa's truck. Fortunately, there's enough food for everybody, and all villagers are fed.

A respectful teenager lends Kotutuwa his bicycle.

This allows the tired Kotutuwa easier travels to Naha's dwelling on the far outskirts of Oraibi.

When Kotutuwa finally arrives at his grandma's adobe, she greets him saying, "Hello, Kotutuwa. How are you holding up?" with a knowing hint of sadness.

Kotutuwa responds in agreement, "My truck has a flat tire that I can't afford to fix. I had to push the truck up to Oraibi, and the people got food. At least I could harvest an abundance of crops today and borrow this bicycle. How do you feel on this crazy day?"

Naha sighs and thoughtfully replies, "I fear for the future. We all saw the Blue Kachina months ago, and the crown virus followed."

Kotutuwa silently nods his agreement and sits the virus safety recommended distance of six feet away from his grandmother. Tonight is perfectly clear, unlike the thick murky clouds and rain that blocked the day's sun. It would be impossible to see anything on this dark, moonless night without the trillions of stars highlighting everything in a ghostly white.

The duo stargazes in silence before Naha says, "The Regime always thought we Indians would be dead by now. But they can't kill us because we are citizens of the stars. Our true home is up there." Naha points toward the sky, and they sadly chuckle. As the laughter dies down, the duo resumes their gaze toward the sky, but their demeanor drastically changes.

Naha and Kotutuwa collapse against cold stone steps in horror. Above them, the ominous sky could cause one to scream, but Kotutuwa and his grandma are stunned into silence, eyes wide with fear. An ominous light forces its way into the heavens and assumes center stage among the planets. This red star is so big and bright that all surrounding white stars reflect a pale pink glow. In the village below, everything looks as if blood was dumped upon the entire village of Oraibi from above.

After the initial shock passes, Kotutuwa hoarsely asks his grandmother, "Is that the Red Kachina?"

Naha slowly faced him solemnly saying, "It is. The end is here."

*****

The police officer seizes Dale and twists his head to the right. Physical domination affords the constable an easy opportunity to cuff and arrest the questionable offender. Instead of following the law, the blue knight kneels on the vulnerable person's neck. Dale chokes and complains, "I can't breathe. Please don't kill me." Unfortunately, his request is denied. Oxygen fails to reach his brain, and his vision blurs. Amid the mounting pain, he manages to say, "I can't breathe" a final time, and these are his last words.

Minutes pass after Dale dies. Yet the blue knight remains on the corpse as if he is a hunted beast, and the murderer is awaiting a trophy from the landlords. Maybe the police officer is merely unaware of the victim's death. Or perhaps the Regime has conditioned descendants of Europe not to care about a Black person's death.

Tonight, we know that one man from Africa was murdered by Regime police. Alas, the murdered man is not just a questionable figure. He is human like the constable who killed him. During his life, this man was a father, a husband, and a loyal employee to his place of work. His name is Dale McHidal, and he is not the first African to be murdered through suffocation in the Regime.

A bright red star suddenly pierces the darkness and startles the blue knight. Everything below is reddened into an ugly wine colored hue, which makes ordinary streets look like war zones.

The police officer suddenly stands stupefied and stiffly stares at the red star. Many explanations can be attributed to this sighting, diminishing the star's significance. But the officer feels as if it shines on his malevolence, broadcasting his wrongdoing. Truth devours the constable, and the reality of murder pierces him deeply. In this icy reality, the police officer accepts that he killed another human being.

People in the Regime have been conditioned to believe that it is justifiable to kill people of African descent. This conditioning manifested itself tonight with the murder of Dale McHidal. The officer who murdered Dale never had an evil thought before. What happened was the byproduct of centuries of genocide, conquest, and forced patriotism.

Shock starts to leave the officer's body, enabling movement. After looking around and over his shoulder, the badged officer scurries to his patrol car, and drives off into the blood-red night.

When the cop drives out of sight, brambles behind the fresh corpse rustle with life. Bea exits them and clings to her phone with a death grip to steady her weeping and shaking body. She wants to scream out in horror from witnessing the slow painful death. But all screams are silenced by intense contempt. The shining star makes the fresh corpse and surrounding buildings shimmer in an angry red color. Bea feels an unseen wrath as if the stars are protesting how the Regime treats people of African descent.

She walks up to the murdered man and films a close-up of his face. Bea then watches the footage of the murder she recorded on her phone and takes pictures of the corpse before uploading them to every social media account she has.

Little does Bea know that her recording is not the full story. But in today's world, news on social media is frequently a half-truth many people insist to be flawless.

After uploading everything to social media, Bea stands and blows the corpse a kiss which is followed by a gust of warm wind. When the gust dies down, clouds again black out the stars. "Goodbye," she whispers before returning home. Unbeknown to Beatrice, she is about to change the world. Unfortunately, this isn't the first time a person of African descent has been murdered in the Regime. Bea is only the second person to record a police officer murdering a person of African descent. The first time someone recorded a similar death no one cared. What will people think now?

FIREWORKS

Last night's video of the police officer murdering the Black man has gone viral across the Regime. That footage has sparked a reservoir of untapped rage in divergent people groups who will come together to unify in protest. Most leaders of the Regime have yet to wake up and watch a replay of the murder on their devices. Soon, the sun will rise and rudely awaken them with the shameful news, for the night when the world saw how the Regime's police treats people of African descent is almost over.

The sun boldly extends its powerful yellow rays, calling all citizens out of bed. Its growing warmth evaporates the remaining thick white clouds from last night's rainstorm. Today is the summer solstice, the longest day of the year. This solstice is particularly pertinent because a series of accidents today will forever alter the Regime.

Dawn has barely passed but thousands of fed up Regime citizens have already started protesting the murder. Scents of sunscreen and sweat fill Regime cities as protestors gather in the sweltering heat on behalf of a stranger who was asphyxiated mere hours ago. Sunshine emboldens protestors like a catalyst for catharsis. However, chaos clouds reason because protestors don't social distance or wear masks while chanting "Black lives matter!" to a dictatorship that appears to believe otherwise.

As is typical for the Regime priorities, profits are valued over the well-being of taxpaying people. Regime rulers benefit too much from racial injustice to reform society, even when citizens want liberty and justice for all. So governors increasingly become enraged over protestors blocking streets, their vital arteries for the flow of money. Much to the landlord's chagrin, protestors livestream their civil disobedience on social media. The world watches live footage of the ongoing unrest of the Regime and scoffs at the government's failure to benefit citizens in the Land of the Free.

Regime's smaller sub-state and city governments use force to silence challengers. Police officers are deployed and wear protective riot gear and armed for their own safety. Yet the precautions protecting constables also dehumanize them. Armor makes people who work in law enforcement look like toy action figures instead of human beings.

Regime police acting as "blue knights" exit their "castle" headquarters prepared to combat the fiery dragons of furious protestors. The opposition lacks weapons and protective gear but has the advantage of a larger presence by way of social media. An observer watching from above might view this new divide in humanity as a living chess match between revolting peasants and the knights who protect the corrupted landlords. Yet the unfolding battle seems rigged when the lordship's armory is compared to the cardboard posters of demands civilians cling to.

Beyond flimsy cardboard shields decorated by colorful markers, the protestors have another advantage the brigades lack. The people who have arrived in protest are not merely protesting a horrific murder. They are exasperated from years of suffering the hidden injustices exposed last night. In retaliation, citizens face off with their greedy governors who still insist they live in the freest and best country ever. Blinded by rage, the avenging tax payers are ready to redress the failures of their empire. For this reason, protestors have nothing to lose, unlike the cops. If anything, the police presence at the front line gives the anguished protestors a direct corporal target.

Police weapons glisten in the sun like talons of a behemoth. Yet protestors stand strong and refuse to surrender. Instead, the law enforcement personnel wrapped in thick, scaly basilisk armor, inspires the rebellion to remain steadfast. Metamorphosis of ordinary people into fearsome blue knights sparks a division within humanity startling protestors into silence. Despite their armor, the seemingly archaic acting coppers can only stare blankly at the civilians whose tax dollars pay their police salaries. Ephemeral silence acts as the unifier for both sides.

Out of the blue, a masked woman who has yet to reach the age of legal adulthood set by the Regime yells, "Black Lives Matter!" Her voice is heard throughout the crowd. As her pleas fades into the wind, the crowd joins in shouting the names of African people who have been murdered by police brutality in the Regime. Although this is but one Regime city, the internet dwarfs the distance between this city's protest and the rest of the world. Citizens across the Regime and world unite by following her lead and shout for racial justice.

Rallying cries of "Black lives matter!" and watching many additional protests on screen devices distracts the rebels from acknowledging the police presence. Out of all bold protestors who refuse to back down, the boldest is a man who has yet to reach forty years of age. However, his Regime-induced habits make him look like an elderly man. While the angry mobs connect over the internet, the man who has lived a sedentary life slowly approaches the police with his empty hands in the air. "Please back down!" police yells in response. Undeterred, he continues approaching until he stands directly in front of a pudgy, pink-faced police officer.

Under the strong sun, all people are sweating heavily and easily lose self-control. Sweat glistens on the skin of police, so they are shiny like a diamond reflecting light. Bulky muscles flex around the guns pointed at protestors. The sun reflecting off armed people makes them resemble marble statues of ancient gods from the old world. Despite appearing godly, all police officers are fearing for their life. In this heat, challengers become sweaty and messy. The clothing of the approaching senior citizen is drenched with sweat as if he had dunked the underarms and sides of his shirt in water. The overpowering sweat produced by the heat and a new fear of civilians decreases the constable's dexterity and weapon safety.

"Please back down!" fearful officers bellow. Undeterred, the brave man stares into the pink-faced constable's watery green eyes and replies, "We are all human and prisoners to the Regime. Our struggles and desires are the same regardless of the sides we are on. Put down your guns, please. Together, we can create a better world for everybody."

The startled green-eyed officer raises his shield preparing for the worse and "Back away!" is bellowed from the brigade.

Contrary to the demands of law enforcement, the bold elderly man grabs a shield and begins lowering it. Startled by the defiance and slippery with sweat, a gun is accidentally fired. Compelled by fear and the loud noise of gun shots, other fingers instinctively pull gun triggers. The ensuing rain of bullets penetrates the protestors' cardboard shields. The senior falls backwards. His death rattle is magnified when his rotund chest lands on a cement curb.

Shocked by this sudden loss of control, constables try to retain authority and yell, "You have been warned. Anyone who comes too close will be prosecuted."

Unfortunately, their commands are overshadowed by a loud unanimous blood-curdling scream from witnesses of the most recent police murder.

In the city of freshly killed rebels, ear-piercing screams shatter the glass windows of surrounding buildings. This horrific sound was broadcast on social media along with footage of bullets penetrating cardboard shields. Distant protestors listening to this noise through headphones also scream in reaction to the unpleasant shock of sound. Their sudden screams shocked those next to them to scream too.

Across the Regime, almost all people are unified by shouting out in horror. Only the police remain silent, and the hairs on their backs stand erect from the horrific shrill. Powerful screams reverberate in everyone's ears and temporarily deafens them. Before the ears of the brigade stopped ringing, protestors aggressively lunge. More shields are forcefully lifted, more guns fired.

Rallied and unified by screams, the protestors attack the police. The aftermath is so gory that the author has chosen to spare the reader from hearing about it. Despite lacking weapons, protestors quickly murder thousands of constables in excruciating ways, even those who did good deeds in the blue uniform.

Guns are taken from dead officers and angry mobs across the Regime shoot up entire cities. A new rallying cry of "Usurp the Regime" is bellowed from fed-up citizens.

Unbeknown to those who are no longer patriotic, their actions mimic the Regime's establishment. Ancestors of today's protestors used to be captives of another country called the Crown. Disgusted by the Crown government, colonizers formed an angry mob and overthrew the world's strongest army of the 1700s. Citizens ungratefully fight the liberty and justice the Regime founding fathers were martyred establishing.

If the ancestors of today's disgruntled citizens usurped the Crown, what are their descendants capable of? The irony is that today's protestors view the Regime the way founding fathers viewed the Crown.

Outside the occupied continent, the Regime colonized a cluster of islands in the Pacific. These islands have been striving to rid themselves of the Regime since its illegal annexation in 1959. The broadcasted sound of countless protestors screaming in unison sparked natives to reestablish the island's ancient kingdom. Military bases and government buildings are bombed and all rude Haoles are sent to sea. These islands are now left to their own methods and crown a questionable queen. But Kapu Aloha to the Regime citizens who treated the indigenous islanders worse than trash.

Back in mainstream society, the scream reverberates in the ears of all. Waves of sound propel reformers forward. The murder of local police and the windows shattered from screams is just the beginning of the riots. Across the Regime, the doors of every building are kicked in. Merchandise in every store is stolen and given to the neglected vagabonds.

Landlords of the Regime hope that the protestors will get tired and stop challenging their authority. If push comes to shove, at least these governors can deploy their secret police to restore order. Usually, the secret police are active after dusk and concealed by the veil of night. These White terrorists vigilantly search for vulnerable Africans to lynch, executing the Regime's dirty deeds for the empire. Towns swarming with secret police stakeouts are therefore nicknamed Sundown Towns because of the dangers these prowlers possess at night. People of African descent warn each other about the safety of Regime towns, saying, "Don't let the sun hit your back here"—by which they mean "Get home safely before the sun sets, or you might die."

Unfortunately for the governors, today is the summer solstice. The planet has orbited in an unfavorable position for the corrupted landlords, providing the serfs with more time to speak out. Most nights, it would be dark by now. At night, people fearfully cower in bed dreaming of a more ethical empire. Currently, the sun hangs in the sky, painting the land red as if the sun has unveiled the Regime's secret and unforgiven past.

There will come a day when every country is forced to atone to the rest of the world for their sins. Today is the day of penance for the Regime. Alas, the sins of the empire are so severe that atonement will last twelve more days.

*****

Destruction encompasses the week following the viral murder and Red Kachina sighting. City and state governments are overrun by scrambled platoons of disorganized mobs attacking the ruling landlords. Despite propaganda and the inundation of unreality TV, citizens have discovered their country's secret, and the government's worst nightmare has become a reality.

All citizens in the Land of the Free suffer from the current chaos. But police are treated the worst. The castle headquarters where blue knights formerly found refuge have been raided and transformed into police-free zones. Cops deployed to restore order are shot at, and Molotov cocktails are thrown in their cruisers. Jails are liberated, and prisoners gratefully join the ranks of protestors. Convicts repay their liberators by avenging law enforcement and perpetuating destruction. Thousands of officers quit their job to escape persecution from citizens and the persistent round-the-clock death threats.

Constables not only fear for their own safety but also their families' safety. Some reformers believe dependents should be punished for the actions of their spouses. These rebels aggressively stalk service members and murder their families in front of them. In some circumstances, the opposition believes that murder isn't a severe enough punishment. Those who fought in undesirable wars or questionable police departments get their houses and cars torched.

Even the dead are forced to atone for their sins. Cemeteries for murderers and invaders the Regime calls heroes are pilfered and transformed into dilapidated construction sites. Rows of formerly immaculate marble tombstones are crushed to white powder. If it weren't for the heat of summer, one would think it snowed in cemeteries across the Regime. Decaying remains of mercenaries are unearthed and strewn across streets swarming with sewage. Passersby stare into gaping holes of empty graves that now resemble portals to the underworld.

Nationwide contamination follows vengeful vandalism. In the early summer heat, the scent of feces, sweat, death, and crumbling buildings form a putrid stench potent enough to stink up the entire world. Monuments to a dwindling democracy are desecrated, while the expanding filth exacerbates the reign of the crown virus.

The restless rebels appear to lack limitations. But each dawn and dusk, their activities are disrupted by a distraction from above. Between day and night, a bloody red star dominates the center sky. Yet each time it shines, it appears farther southwest than before. When this strange star manifests, all people can do is stare blankly and marvel at its haunting ethereal beauty. Only after it is veiled by night or diminished by daylight does the destruction continue.

Patriotism is now a rarity. Most patriots hide their continued loyalties to the Regime. Yet one bold group is determined to make order last longer than the appearance of a strange star. These are the White knights, the Regime's secret police. Tonight, they will conduct a private meeting about restoring order and quelling the insurrection. As is typical for the secret police, any measures of force needed to strengthen the Regime's reign will be employed. They believe themselves to be above and beyond the law. Unbeknown to these white knights, their next move will be their last.

* * * * *

A group of ordinary citizens garbed in street clothes gather in pews. There are few shadows in the harshly lit room, creating the illusion that there are no secrets here. Ironically, these people compose a battalion of the Regime's secret police. This room is fittingly decorated with Regime flags and nooses. It feels impossible to number the stars from the many flags hanging here. Yet stars and stripes are outnumbered by a religious icon commemorating a prophet who believed people should love each other regardless of race. The leader who calls himself an imperial wizard stands, facing pews of seated white knights in this room of hideous and incorrectly referenced decorum.

The imperial wizard who lacks magic clears his throat with a low growling noise. Next, he addresses the people in attendance, "I greet you, fellow knights. You have been summoned to the Klavern tonight because we must declare war on the African uprising and our fellow 100 percenters who have become race traitors by siding with inferior races. As White knights, it is our duty to protect our race, the best race, and uphold the sovereignty of the Regime." Overcome by a brutal coughing fit, the wizard stops speaking.

After excreting yellow phlegm in a white tissue, the wizard continued drawling in his slow monotone voice, "I have spent my past few days talking with imperial wizards across the Regime. Everyone I've spoken to concludes that order must be restored at any cost. Unfortunately, our dispatch, the blue knights, is being murdered in brutal ways. It is now our responsibility to restore order and return police authority. Inferior races and race betrayers have become stronger than ever. When we face them, we face death.

We restore order *non silba sed anthar*. Congregants agree and define the wizard's slogan as "Not self, but others." The magicless wizard continues, "With help from the sacred unfailing being, all squadrons of White knights will unite tomorrow at midnight and take back the land. It is our responsibility to make the Regime white again. To do that, we must keep this plan secret, and as of tomorrow, normalcy will be restored. For god race and nation!"

The imperial wizard sat down to signal that he was done speaking. In response, the congregation of White knights chanted, "For god race and nation!" The meeting was adjourned with shrills of "White power!" Shortly after returning home, the imperial wizard texted allies about the successful meeting and went to bed confident in his plan. Unbeknown to him, some of the White Knights went drinking right after the meeting and spilled the secret plan.

* * * * *

A person with short green hair rushes out of a bar and drunkenly trips on an uprooted sidewalk. In their current state of mind, they question the validity of some overheard drunken jabber.

Regardless, the luxury of time doesn't exist when fascists threaten to rise again. The fearful drunk manages to access a cellphone and contact others who hate the White knights. Shortly thereafter, the regional manager of White-knight haters, called the fearless leader, invites people to join an urgent meeting.

Hours pass before random people donned in red and black pants with black tops sit in concentric circles on the floor of an ink-black room. These are Black knights, the fiercest opposition to White knights. Despite forming a secret society, no one doubts the existence of the White knights because they regularly lynch racial minorities and burn icons of their faith at barbeques. Yet the Black knights make such rare appearances that Regime citizens question their existence.

In this dark room, the Black knights can't even see each other. What matters most to them is what others can see, not what they see. The silent, dark atmosphere is broken by a deep voice, reminding people, "Chaos isn't a pit. Chaos is a ladder. This past week has been filled with nothing but destruction to a dictator-ship-occupying Indigenous soil. We have used this time of chaos to share banned literature shining more light on the parasitic Regime. Thus far, blue knights have been executed and prisoners liberated. These events have acted as a vehicle for the destruction of unfair-ness. However, recent circumstances threaten to end this trend."

The speaker paused to lend others the opportunity to talk. The person with green hair who fearfully fled the bar hours ago told everyone, "Not long ago, I encountered some White knights. They were drinking, so I don't know the full truth about their threats. However, they might make a murderous appearance; and unless we act, many people will die because of it. You have come here tonight because you are uncertain about what to do, or perhaps you don't know the full extent of power White knights possess. But why allow these knights who are in power to rob us and oth-ers step by step, openly and in secret, until nothing will remain but them? I propose that tomorrow, one minute after midnight, we fight and eliminate these horrific White knights forever. Any suggestions?"

The room fell quiet before a person in attendance asked, "Wouldn't we succumb to the ethics of the White knights if we used their tactics of horror against them?"

This interesting question sank into the minds of all.

In response, a person masked by darkness with a scratchy shrilly voice asked, "Has your mind been too imprisoned by the Regime to the point where you forgot it is your moral obligation to eliminate this system of racism and genocide?" In response, the question poser reminded everyone that, "We are supposed to be as peaceful as possible. How can we be certain that killing White knights is the answer?"

More silence in the dark room before the person with the bold, deep voice answered, "Tomorrow at midnight, White knights will use lethal force upon many people who will die. We have spent years in peace trying hard to stop these White knights through rea-son, logic, the passage of literature, and lobbying of our landlords.

Unless we act against the White knights with strength and force tomorrow, many will die. We will therefore be responsible for the deaths of thousands because we knew the White knights would rise to power and murder many, but we did nothing to stop them."

This reasoning seemed good to everyone.

Yet to strengthen resolve, a person who is usually quiet reminded everyone in a soft voice, "We fight evil by sharing literature, so we don't have to fight it verbally. We fight evil verbally, so we don't have to fight it with fists. We fight evil with fists, so we don't have to fight it with knives. We fight evil with guns when evil would otherwise murder the innocent."

Everyone nodded in agreement even though they didn't see others nod in unison.

Silence settled again, until the deep voice reminded the opposition, "You are all free to choose what you do tomorrow at one minute past midnight. But to be effective, we must be serious about tomorrow. I will pass out pieces of paper and pens. Before this meeting adjourns, please write an X on a piece of paper, and leave it folded on the floor if you promise to face off against the White knights. In addition to promising your presence, please write an X next to any flammable materials you may have in your home or are able to acquire before one minute past midnight tomorrow. And whatever you do next, be safe but not silent!"

The meeting was adjourned, all that was left were pieces of paper with scribbled X's and notes about what flammable materials attendees had.

* * * * *

Summer solstice passed twelve nights ago, so the days are getting shorter. Dark dust clouds from the rubble and crumbled cement augment the shortening days by blocking the sun. The few remaining streetlights shine all the time. Their faint glow in the perpetual dusk creates the pattern of a chessboard.

While most places in the Regime have been transformed into chessboard-like patterns, tonight we focus on the most volatile place, the capitol. In this abysmal atmosphere, tall people garbed like white candles patrol block 800D with a regal gait. Fortified in the white castle at 800H, the landlord waits for the White knights to restore order. Compared to flickering streetlights, White knight robes are reliable light. For this reason, protestors see them approaching with guns and run to the safe space on block 300A.

Hooded crowns limit visibility, yet the knights see the protestors scatter. Protestors are like pawns because they can only move one block at a time. Pawns with good intentions are vulnerable to adroit knights who traverse the kingdom freely with routes most citizens will never know. Furthermore, each White knight carries a rifle. None of the protestors have firearms, which heightens their endangerment.

Fortunately, something lurking in the dark night goes undetected by White knights. Black knights, the strongest competitor, hide in deep shadows tonight.

Index fingers are placed on gun triggers as White knights get giddy chasing protestors. Racial slurs and other horrific venom are released from their mouths, and shadows are desperately searched for people to lynch. The White knights are so focused on whitewashing Native American land that they fail to notice rebellious forces until "Surprise!"

After fearlessly traveling two blocks diagonally, the White knights stand stupefied in front of the building addressed B666. Only five buildings away, Black knights yelled "Surprise!" while waving flaming torches. Normally, Black knights are invisible at night because their dark uniforms provide sufficient camouflage. Tonight, the White knights fear their worst nightmare is about to come true and place the rebels in check by aggressively shooting at the black block.

Torches held by the now slaughtered black knights slip out of their cold hands on defaced buildings that immediately go up in flames. Realizing that they only made their nightmare more probable, White knights panic and sprint to B300. Beneath the hoods, everyone flushes red with shame and fear. Another course of action will be needed tonight for victory. Dumbly, White knights turn their White backs on the dark night and huddle together in a circle to discuss options.

Unbeknown to the White knights, some members of the black block survived the shooting. The survivors fled to guard the safe space at A300 which backs into the enemies' current location. Without torches, the residual rebellion remains invisible. Stepping in silence and barely breathing, the Black knights form a human chain around the White knights. Eager to fight fire with fire, they remove cans of hairspray from their baggy hoodie pockets. Due to the limited peripheral vision created by hooded crowns, oppressors fail to see small flames sparked from cigarette lighters. When they hear the hiss of hairspray and finally see fire, they realize their worst nightmare has come true and it's too late to flee.

Hairspray transforms small flames into infernos. The flames engulf white robes creating human torches. Blood-curdling screams of anguish ensue from White knights who are being treated the way they have treated people from Africa for centuries. The cacophony of screaming White supremacists temporarily deafens the black block. Before their ears stop ringing, the volatile robes of White knights explode like a bomb and conflagration follows.

From above, this explosion is observed by satellites recording an orange eruption of flames. The perpetual night of the Regime is broken by a sea of voracious flames gorging on defaced buildings. Knights from both sides and protestors are the first to die from the combustion.

The inferno at the capitol picks up steam while it travels. The more buildings it burns, the hotter it gets. The hotter it gets, the more fearsome it becomes. All roads in the Regime lead to Columbus. Unfortunately for Regime citizens, roads in the capitol have caught fire. Blazes traverse the Regime infrastructure like a river in hell killing millions. The Black knights had good intentions when challenging the White knights. However, millions of innocent deaths prove that people should not fight fire with fire.

Back in 800H, the White landlord remains fortified. Alas, the fortifications failed to protect him from expansive flames. All oxy-

gen has been combusted in the atmosphere resulting in fast suffocation. Instead of perishing in anguish like the taxpaying citizens,
a smile crosses his face. Most corpses are obliterated by flames,
but the forty-fifth president's corpse smiles as if this is all a joke.

Today is the fourth of July. Two centuries ago, on July fourth,
the birth certificate of the Regime was signed. Annually on July
fourth, the Regime has a birthday party celebrated by an artful
display of fireworks. Tonight, fireworks are being expelled, but
they are not nice to witness. Tonight's fireworks make the remains
of the Regime look like hell, for all Regime soil is on fire, and the
Regime's secret police have been obliterated.

THE AFTERMATH

Today is a new day. The inferno has passed and I sit alone in the predawn darkness near the edge of a cliff that towers above thick, stifling smoke. My hair is full of ash, and my skin is darkened from sooty air. Soon, I will occupy myself the same way I have for the past four days.

Gripping a nail that survived the incineration of the neighboring Verhoogen mansion, a souvenir of my past life, I write about the conflagration I survived. Don't ask what country I am in because I no longer know. But since I am on the third mesa, the center of the universe, does it really matter what political boundaries surround me?

I stumbled here after days of coughing up blood and searching for clean air to breathe. To be honest, I don't know how anybody survived such an unexpected and devastating inferno. All I remember is leaving my residence for a quick walk. Outside, a wall of flames greeted me. Panicked and not thinking clearly, I charged toward the eagle-shaped fountain in front of the town hall submersing myself in the water and hoped for the best.

I don't remember anything about the blaze. So I must have repressed memories of the event. Consciousness returned only after the raging fire had reduced shiny buildings and amber waves of grain to ash and then dissipated. When I saw the town where I was residing transformed into an extinguished hell, all I could do was scream and sob uncontrollably.

Eventually, my throat became raw from screaming and my body fatigued from crying. In a weary state of mind, I stood up and searched for human survivors. Animals abound and strangely appear to be in perfect health. It's as if the blaze knew they were innocent and undeserving of punishment. Searching under a sky darkened from burnt buildings increased the difficulty of finding human life amid the destruction. All I encountered had perished in the fire. Their charred bodies were unrecognizable.

After three weeks of desperately digging through the rubble for survivors, my health deteriorated, forcing me to abandon my efforts or die. An indescribable premonition guided me away from the toxic town. My travels took me through a desert and past Anasazi ruins which were untouched by flames. Eventually, I stood at the foot of the third mesa and peered up. When I failed to see the summit beyond the smoke, I decided that the mesa was the healthiest place for me and ascended. Currently, my greatest desire is to find fellow survivors. But today is my fifth day here, and I have yet to find anything remotely reminiscent of human existence.

It feels like yesterday I participated in a Fourth of July parade by gorging on sickeningly sweet candies and waving Regime flags. In reality, all flags I waved back then, along with everything else celebrated, has been incinerated in a blaze. From this experience, I learned that power and wealth only delay the fact that every action has an opposite but equal reaction. Suffering from an inferno was the penance we the people paid to atone for the sins of our ancestors. If only my predecessors hadn't invaded and pilfered the Americas, descendants of Europe may have been spared from the conflagration.

But what readers think about my records is beyond my control. All I can do is write and hope for the best. I don't know if any other empires have crumbled like the Regime. Alas, those who do not learn from the past are doomed to repeat it, for the devastation that overcame the Regime can happen anywhere. Citizens of the world ought not to invade Indigenous lands or disrespect indigenous people. Such actions endanger invaders to perish in a fire like the inferno that liberated Native Americans from the Regime.

When I finish writing this history, I will stash my notes in a crevasse within Prophecy Rock. There, it will be protected from the elements yet easy for future generations to find. I am surprised that the grand empire from my youth has been reduced to rubble. But those who come after me will view the notes I am currently writing as nothing more than a page in history to be read or ripped out.

The Hopi prophesized a grand destruction long before my birth. If the conflagration I just survived is the purification prophesized, is it really a bad event, or are there benefits I have yet to experience?

These questions churn in my mind. But of all burning questions, the most pressing is this: Where are the Hopi? Their prophecy predicted that some people would remain. Survivors of the great fire are prophesized to have saved themselves from the mind trap of Regime patriotism. Such people are kind, noble, peaceful, well-mannered, and eager to attain knowledge. During the reign of the Regime, skeptical citizens were treated maliciously. Ironically, I survived the fire with them for reasons I can't comprehend. All I can do now is hope that I am not alone in this dead empire where ashes fall like snow. The sun is finally up. I must continue writing.

Snap! Out of nowhere, my attention is diverted from scribbling to a snapping stick on the mesa. I turn my head toward the source of sound and am relieved to see two men in ethnic clothes approaching me. The man on the left wears a white button-down shirt over blue jeans with moccasins laced up to his knees. He is adorned with a silver concho belt and a necklace of turquoise stones. Strands of defiant-grey hair poke out from behind his black headband. The other man is barefoot but garbed in a knee-length brown skirt topped by a red poncho with white tribal patterns. He has dark, shoulder-length hair and short bangs.

Relieved that I am not alone, I turn toward the approaching men. As they come closer, I hear bits of their conversation.

"Well, the *biligana* (Dinè word for White person) finally did it!" the man with gray hair says before sighing.

"Yes, they did, and that is unfortunate. I had always hoped Europeans would change their ways before everyone suffered so much. But they were so obsessed with their flickering devices that they didn't even see the mistakes they were making."

The man in white frowned in response and agreed. "Very sad. But apparently, people can only resist your tribe's prophecy for so long. I just wish it hadn't come to this. But the mainstream citizens were warned and chose to ignore all of us."

The man in the poncho frowned and said, "Yes. It is sad that so many suffered. But now, everything in the Regime has been purified. I don't know what is to come. Let's just hope that this next realm of existence is one where all people are treated better than how the Regime treated us and other non-Europeans."

The man in white nodded in agreement and both people continued walking in silence.

The man in the poncho broached another conversation, "It's funny how we were both so fearful that the crown virus would obliterate our tribes. Instead, it saved us from an unfair regime that has hurt trillions."

I stood up from behind the rock where I was writing and repeated a phrase I heard long ago. "Still, a more glorious dawn awaits. Not a sunrise but a galaxy rise."

The walkers looked at me sternly before asking, "Who are you? What are you doing up here?"

I showed them my notebook and replied, "Writing history."

The man on the right gently grabbed my notes while smiling.

The man on the left solemnly stared at me while asking, "Are you a lost Native?"

"No. I'm European," I answered.

He chuckled before asking, "Well then, how did you know to come here?"

I looked at the earth below the mesa and saw nothing but smoke. Then I replied, "I hoped that this vantage point would enable me to see people below. I really hoped that I was not the sole survivor."

Both men were silent for a moment.

The man in the white shirt said, "I think the crown virus has finally died. We thought our two tribes were all who survived. Do you know where your family is? Where do you live?"

I avoided looking into their dark eyes and thought about the expansive flames, which engulfed the country I was conditioned to love.

Apparently, my distress was visible despite my best efforts to conceal it. The man in white softly said, "Come here. You are welcome to stay with us. I'm glad you survived."

The man in the poncho asked me, "How did you get up here?"

"I climbed."

"How did you *know* to come up here?"

I paused before answering in a low, awkward voice, "I read the Hopi prophecy during my scheduled reading time, and it said to."

Both men stared at me before conversing in a language I don't know while pouring over the notes I had scribbled.

After reading my notes, they looked at me sternly and said, "You need to come with us."

Before agreeing to the demands of strangers, I asked, "Who are you, people?"

The duo laughed at my question, and the man in the white shirt answered first in his native tongue before saying, "I am Jim Sweetwater. A Dinè elder and medicine man."

The short man in the poncho said, "My name is Kotutuwa Nawasha, and I am a Hopi maize farmer."

I didn't know what to say, so I remained silent as we walked across yellow sand and past pale-green shrubs.

Jim started another conversation. "I heard you mention the Hopi Prophecy. I guess you know a little bit about the Hopi. Do you know about my tribe the Dinè?"

"No," I answered.

"Well, you probably do but don't know it. We Dinè are actually listed as being Navajo by the Regime. Have you heard of the Navajo?"

I remember something I heard long ago about some Navajo people who made a code to invade and pilfer another country like what the Regime did to them. After failing to find a nice way to phrase that, I replied, "I'm not sure."

Before anyone could say anything else, we arrived at the base of the mesa, and I came face to face with more people in ethnic clothes.

The new people eagerly approached us and one of them asked, "Who did you find?"

I became overwhelmed by their presence after a month alone and didn't want to talk anymore. Jim may have picked up on my anxiety because he answered for me. I retreated as the crowd walked toward us. Just as I was about to sprint back up the mesa, Jim blocked me, so I was face to face with the new people. Everyone appeared to pick up on my uneasiness in dealing with things I am not used to. The strangers stopped looking at me and turned their gazes to Jim and Kotutuwa.

Nevertheless, their curiosity was at full force, and they quietly asked me, "What's your name? What did you experience?"

I answered their questions slowly and without eye contact, but they listened with eager patience.

When I was done answering their questions, Kotutuwa decided, "Let's wait for more people to come hear what she wrote about."

Kotutuwa gave me flatbread that tasted like corn. Apparently, it's a Hopi food called piki bread. I also drank water out of a tribal-patterned jug, another new thing. In my past life, I would refuse to drink from anything but my specific ceramic mug. However, this past month has altered my perception of what is acceptable.

"Do you like the paintings on the jug?" Kotutuwa asked.

I shook my head no.

He either didn't notice or didn't care because he continued saying, "We Hopi paint to tell a story. This story talks about a time of great drought that withered many crops. People prayed intensely for rain, and when it came, all of their needs were met."

I liked the story and began to like the jug too.

Thousands of people gathered in front of me, all of whom were dressed in Native American regalia.

Jim addressed everyone saying, "Dear people, we do not know what is ahead of us. What we do know is that our fate will change. Whether it is for better or worse has yet to be seen."

Naha added, "It appears that the Hopi Prophecy has been fulfilled! All remaining people will be kind and humble. Now that evil is gone, we can stand up and take back what is ours. But the earth is really hurting from this destruction, and we must help her heal."

People looked intensely at me, and I sank away from their gaze. They refused to look away from me, so I reluctantly looked up.

Kotutuwa smiled at me and announced, "We have all spent the past month searching for survivors outside our tribes. Today, when Jim and I searched the third mesa, we met this woman. She has been observant of the behavior of people in the pandemic and the ensuing conflagration. We would like her to share her observations with us."

I stood up ready to share my findings with the eager audience. Still recovering from all the smoke, I took another sip of water before speaking. After skimming my notebook, I decided to give everyone a summary of my observations, "I don't really know what happened. It seems like the protestors started a fire that got out of hand, became an inferno, and spread everywhere. Millions of people were killed in the blaze. In fact, death and destruction were so prolific in my former city that I actually believed myself to have died and gone to hell. In desperation, I searched for survivors. After three weeks of searching, I lost my sense of smell, and my lungs felt raw from breathing the smoke. The pollution was so bad that I had to leave or die. I traveled to the mesas, hoping to access fresh air above the smoke while continuing my search for survivors below. I am so happy to find all of you on my fifth day of camping here! Before meeting Jim and Kotutuwa this morning, I believed myself to be the sole survivor of the Regime!"

I smiled and bowed to the audience who applauded my speech. For reasons I can't comprehend, I then broke down sobbing uncontrollably in front of thousands of strangers.

I do not remember what happened next. What I do remember is being awakened by songs in Dinè Bizaad language the morning after inside a circular dwelling of wood and clay. The people who awoke me then said that I can stay with them. Together, we exited the *Hogan* and ran from east to west while sprinkling yellow corn pollen and singing to the new day.

The following week was filled with my difficult acclimation to a new normal. Before the Regime was destroyed, my life was structured around my self-planned activities. I would arrange to see certain people and go to specific places at scheduled times on predetermined days. I would scream and become distraught over any change to my meticulously planned schedule! My Dinè roommates don't share my views on the importance of schedules and are laid-back when completing tasks. Exposure to their different outlook on time and purpose, paired with no running water, electricity, or internet had me really upset. Beyond learning to live without things I am used to, I had to deal with other things I hate.

For instance, I am not a morning person. Unfortunately for me, the Dinè rise before dawn, and they expect me to join them. I also don't like dirt, but my Dinè friends expects me to help them farm. I angrily lashed out about doing things I hate in ways my family didn't appreciate. To be honest, I am surprised that I have not been exiled from Dinètah yet.

After my initial culture shock and adjustment to a more strenuous life, I am finally happy. I am more content in Dinètah, the real Navajo Nation, than I ever was in the comfortable confines of my former institution. My new life is filled with farming and learning the Dinè Bizaad language. However, I feel obligated to ensure that future governments never make the mistakes I once benefited from. To do that, I began writing the book you are currently reading.

Dinè culture has recovered from colonization like a phoenix rising from ashes. European clothing is no longer worn. Today's Dinè only wear traditional regalia with long hair in traditional buns. Dinè Bizaad is no longer endangered because everyone dwelling in Dinètah is required to learn and speak the Navajo language. English is only spoken in business exchanges with other tribal nations and the rest of the other continents. All temples for deities created by Europeans were destroyed in the blaze. Missionaries are a thing of the past because traditional beliefs abound.

Shortly after my arrival, Dinètah received an unseasonal week-long downpour. Rain washed away smoke, so the Dinè could see and connect with other tribes. Shortly thereafter, expansive pre-Columbian trade routes were reestablished.

Trade has given the Dinè and Hopi peoples the economic stability desired but not afforded to them during the reign of the Regime. From what I've observed during business exchanges and friendly visits with other tribal nations, they too are blossoming. Everyone celebrates the return to pre-Columbian normalcy. However, all tribes make the earth's health the biggest priority. In fact, knowledge of the land is the biggest commodity in trade, which is shared freely for the benefit of all.

The biggest part of restoration revolves around "seed libraries," or archives for crop seeds. Most archives cataloged the plants Native Americans relied upon before European invasions. Natives raided seed libraries after the conflagration destroyed barriers to the archives. The cataloged inventory is being returned to and replanted in its natural habitat. Preparing the soil for planting requires removing rubble and digging. While digging, sad mysteries deemed insolvable during the reign of the Regime are finally solved.

Unmarked graves for murdered indigenous women are unearthed. The victim's corpses are respectfully returned to their tribal lands where they receive their last rites. Underground holding cells for surviving trafficked women are uncovered, and the captives are liberated. Tribal nations are now the leading global force in ending human trafficking.

Each day, the survivors of the Regime become happier as the chains of European domination deteriorate. In my life, I have never been around people as happy as those I am currently with. A new seaport is being constructed to enable international trade. All shipments will be meticulously searched for more missing women.

Most murdered or missing Indigenous women have returned home dead or alive. But there is still one lost woman who is a member of the Hopi Nation. Each shipment that arrives in the new seaport is scoured for her. Other trafficked women have been liberated from their abductors. Survivors of human trafficking chose to either return to their homeland or join a tribal nation. Gratitude from freed sex slaves is abundant.

The neighboring Hopis are fervently preparing for the holiest time of the year, the Snake Dance. This year's Snake Dance is extra special because it is the first in centuries to not be performed under occupation. Four days before the preparations are complete, everything is postponed to celebrate a positive ending to centuries of exploitation.

A cargo ship has anchored at the port. Employees scour each cargo container to ensure every shipment received is fit for the land. One of the shipments contain trafficked women of all races and ages. Of the many women, one of them is Hopi, the last missing Indigenous woman.

Hopis chose to conduct the Snake Dance after welcoming her home. People from other tribes celebrate with the Hopi, rejoicing in the fact that there are no more trafficked sisters. News of the homebound route the Hopi woman travels through trade routes. Nations surrounding her route home prepare gifts and healing ceremonies for her to enjoy while passing through. They shower her with positivity to help her heal from years of enslavement.

After a fortnight of traveling, the found Hopi woman will finally arrive home today! Neighboring tribes such as the Utes, other Puebloans, some People of the Plains, and of course, the Dinè camp below the third mesa to welcome her home. People representing their tribes in colorful regalia dot the sprawling red desert with their teepees. Together we fill the air with healing songs from Indigenous languages.

Two elders I now live with asked me to refer to them as my Dinè grandparents. They have instructed me to sing for her in Dinè Bizaad:

This is your home, my grandchild!
My grandchild, I have returned with you to your home,
Upon the pollen figure I have returned
to sit with you, my grandchild.
Your homes are yours again. Your fire is yours again. Your food
is yours again. Your mountains are yours again, my grandchild.

The final returning Hopi is escorted by her family up the black mesa. Other Hopis dressed like Kachinas waft sweetgrass toward her in greeting. When she reaches the summit, the sky turns bright red. It is high noon, so we know this red sky is not created by the setting sun. This strange change to the sky distracts us from singing, and all we can do is look upward in startled silence. Shooting stars traverse the red sky leaving a trail of rainbow stardust.

All is silent until *BOOM*!

A supersonic boom reverberates across the desert landscape, temporarily deafening me and knocking me flat on my back. When I open my eyes, the sky has transformed from red to black. Everything appears black under the now-starless sky, except for a bright-red figure descending to earth. I have no words to describe this thing except that it is red, stands upright, and is short like most Hopis. I have no idea what it is, nor do I know what others think because everyone remains silent.

Is this the Red Kachina landing on the third mesa? Does this signify the setting right of all wrongs perpetrated against Native Americans, or maybe this whole experience is just an extravagant dream? Maybe Native Americans are still suffering and their longed-for freedom and healing continue to elude them. What will I see when I wake up?

EPILOGUE

Thank you for reading my book.

Please know that the stories behind written pages are inspired by real events and people. Therefore, each character you have come to know has suffered both figuratively and literally. Unfortunately, the unfairness described in this book is but a snippet of what Native Americans actually endure on a daily basis.

The author has written this specific snipped about a pandemic of suffering from three main objectives. Firstly, raising awareness. Most people take their citizenship in the Regime for granted and ignore the fact that they reside in a dictatorship. Likewise, too many people turn a blind eye to the racism, which founded and perpetuates America's existence. Both behaviors hurt millions of people. Yet patriots are simply unaware of the damage they inflict or the true meaning behind the flags they raise in their yards.

Secondly, empowerment. The Regime's economy profits from humiliating racial minorities for their immutable characteristics. But everyone is beautiful in their own right. The main characters in this book are racial minorities because the author hopes that the positive representation of historically overlooked people will help them feel seen and heard.

Thirdly, encouragement. It takes courage to speak out against one's home country. Continuously doing the right thing in the wrong empire can tire citizens, especially when they are punished for speaking out. who do the right thing in the wrong empire despite the initial appearance. Millions of citizens risked their own safety to demand justice for Dale McHidal, a man the protestors never knew. By standing up for Dale despite repercussions from the Regime, protestors became the epitome of altruism. Some people might think those protestors are sinister and vile because they burned down the Regime. They are correct because fighting fire with fire always results in countless unpleasant deaths. In the end, those same protestors wound up saving future generations, which could amount to trillions of people from being murdered by police.

It is the author's hope that readers will be inspired to do what is right and help others. So what you chose to do next is entirely up to you.

If you wish to pursue more knowledge of topics you enjoyed in this book, then proceed to the "Bibliography" and "Further Reading" sections. If you lack interest in reading further, you can still change our world for the better.

A reader who holds a position of political power can honor treaties with the Indigenous people in their area. Yet ordinary humans like myself can still be a catalyst for change through kindness. For kindness shines through one's misfortune like a ray of hope. Kind people stand out in a world swarming with selfishness. Besides, it is the author's hope that a day will come when the benevolent outnumber the greedy. Until that day comes, all we can do is be kind and hope for the best.

The real end has yet to come, but we still have the power to remedy the mistreatment of Native Americans. In making wrongs right, not only are we benefiting others but we also benefit ourselves. We, too, suffer on behalf of our own actions.

Walk in beauty always.

Fin.

IMAGES

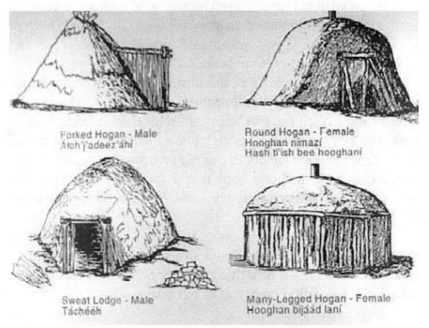

Forked Hogan - Male
Atch'į'adeez'áhí

Round Hogan - Female
Hooghan nímazí
Hash tł'ish bee hooghaní

Sweat Lodge - Male
Táchééh

Many-Legged Hogan - Female
Hooghan bijáád łání

Picture of the different traditional Dinè houses called *Hogans*. The female *Hogan* was used for living, the round *Hogan* was lived in during winters, and the many-legged *Hogan* was lived in during summers. The male *Hogan* is used for ceremonial purposes or sweat lodges to cleanse oneself.

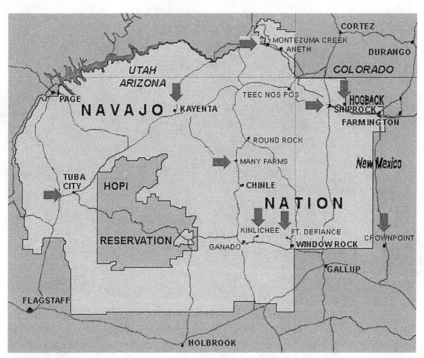

A map of the Navajo Nation today in relation to surrounding states, cities, and the Hopi Nation.

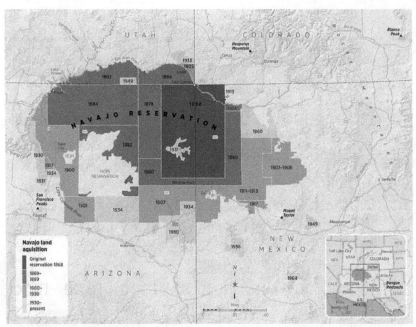

A map showing the successful Dinè land reclamation. The original Navajo Nation granted in the Treaty of 1868 is a 90 percent reduction of Dinè ancestral land and is shown in the color purple. The most recent land reclamations are shown in pale yellow. While this land reclamation is quite successful, the Dinè have yet to take back the entirety of their aboriginal land because ancestral Dinè land consists of all land between Mount Taylor, Mount Blanca, Hesperus Mountain, and the San Francisco Peaks, which are all shown on this map.

This is today's flag of the Navajo Nation. The dark square in the middle is the original reservation of 1886. The other divisions etched into today's Navajo Nation show the addition of other successfully acquired land. The four mountains surrounding the Navajo Nation of today represent the four sacred mountains showing the extent of the true aboriginal Dinè land.

This picture displays the Navajo Nation flag over the flag of the Regime with Geronimo on it. This flag is placed in the far north of the Navajo Nation. The land beyond these flags is still occupied by the Regime despite being ancestral Dinè land.

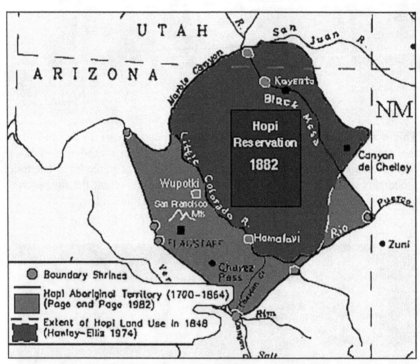

This map shows the ancestral land of the Hopi people in a light red color, which the Hopi have lost to the Dinè. As can be seen on this map, many Hopi shrines now reside in the Navajo Nation. The darker red color in the middle was a joint-use area for both Navajo and Hopi people, but the darkest red square marks the original Hopi Nation of 1882.

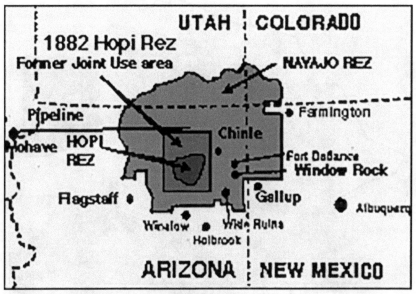

This map shows the consequences the Navajo Hopi joint use area had on the losing of Hopi ancestral land. The dotted lines running through the center of this map are the boundaries of neighboring states, and the biggest mass of red in this map is of the current Navajo Nation. The square area in the middle of the Navajo Nation was the original Hopi Nation of 1882, which later became a joint-use area between the Navajo and Hopi people but is now part of the Navajo Nation. The smallest, dark-red dot in the middle of the red square is the Hopi Nation of today. From this map, one can see how much ancestral land the Hopi people have lost since 1882.

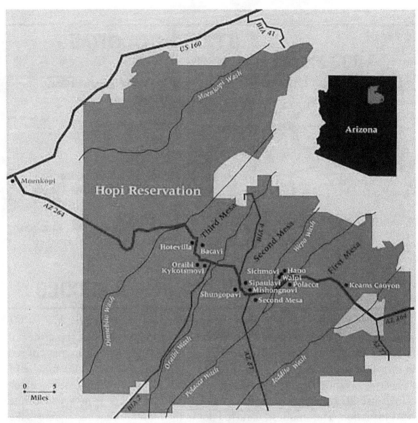

A geographically accurate map of the Hopi Nation today. This map shows the shape of the Hopi Nation, where it resides in the state of Arizona and where each Hopi village is in relation to the three mesas.

The great variety of Hopi maize.

The flag of the Hopi Nation showcases the diversity of maize the Hopi people have cultivated and having maize on a flag shows how significant it is to the Hopi people.

Some Hopi Kachina dolls.

Conquistadors meeting Arawak and Carib peoples who are indigenous to the Caribbean Islands.

The pyramids of Mesoamerica are one of many building feats accomplished before the arrival of Columbus. These pyramids, like most ancient American buildings, are made entirely of stacked stones held together without mortar or cement. Before European invasions, life was abundant on the American continents. Over eight hundred thousand people lived in the area, now called Honduras and El Salvador at the time of Columbus's arrival, yet this empire didn't have the challenges of sanitation or civil unrest, which was normal in Europe during this time. The ability to build grand fortresses like this, despite being isolated from the shared knowledge of the old world, reveals the true genius of Native Americans. On a sidenote, Columbus didn't visit the Mayan Empire in 1492 as the author suggests but went there on his fourth and final voyage in 1502. The author has blurred the timeline and routes of Columbus only to make the story more interesting. If you wish to learn more information, go to the "Further Reading" section.

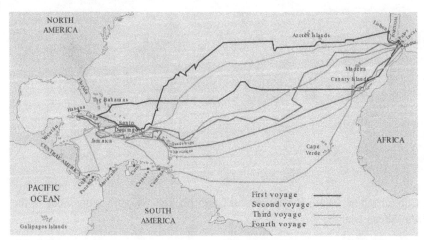

This is a map of Columbus's voyages. The author blurred the timelines and actual routes of travel to make the story a bit more interesting.

Kindred Spirits is the title of this painting that shows the charity Native Americans gave to Ireland during the potato famine. While many tribes including the Dinè selflessly helped the Irish, the Choctaw Nation donated the most resources. For that reason, the Choctaw are depicted in this painting.

This monument in Cork, Ireland, was erected in 2006 to honor the help many Native American tribes gave the Irish people during the Great Hunger from 1845–1857. This monument has Choctaw symbolism because that tribal nation provided the greatest charitable relief. But the Irish government repaid other helpful tribes and also donated to the Navajo Hopi COVID-19 fund.

the Territory of New Mexico at their
hands and seals.

W. T. Sherman
Lt Genl,
                Indian Peace Commissioner
S. F. Tappan,
                Indian Peace Commissioner

Barboncito   Chief   his X mark
Delgadito   his X mark
Armijo   his X mark
  Delgado
Manuelito   his X mark
Largo   his X mark
Herrero   his X mark
Chiquito   his X mark
Muerto de Hombre   his X mark
Hombro   his X mark
Narbono   his X mark
Narbono segundo   his X mark
Ganado Mucho   his X mark
                    Council

This is a picture of the original Treaty of 1868 signatures. Notice they are all
signed with an "X" because none of the treaty signers understood English well
in 1868.

IMAGE CREDITS

1. *Shelter. Great Basin Native Americans.* Weebly. 890882723646632447.weebly.com/shelter.html.
2. Baca, Angelo. *Map of the Navajo Nation. Into America the Ancestor's Land.* WordPress, October 25, 2015, intoamericafilm.wordpress.com/the-dine-land-and-resources/.
3. *Navajo Nation Land Acquisition. Cartographic Concepts.* Smithsonian Institute, 2020, www.mapmanusa.com/ images/exhibit-maps/smithsonian-NMAI-navajo-land-aquisitions.jpg.
4. *DiscoverNavajoHistory.com.* Navajo Tourism Department, 2020, www.discovernavajo.com/uploads/ images/NaFlag(1).jpg.
5. *Getty Images.* media.gettyimages.com/photos/navajonation-flag-and-modified-american-flag-with-end-of-the-trail-picture-id1060150644?s=612x612.
6. *Navajo Hopi Land Dispute. Hanksville.net*, March 20, 1997, hanksville.net/maps/az/navhopi.html.
7. Nobles, Tom M. *Hopi Reservation. TomNobles.com*, July 28, 2013. www.tomnobles.com/Subject_Directory/ Research/Prophecy_Prophets/images/Map.jpg.
8. Crow Canyon Archeological Center. *The Diversity of Hopi Maize. Pueblo Farming Project of Crow Canyon Archeology Center.* History Colorado, Colorado State Historical Fund, 2017. pfp.crowcanyon.org/results.html.
9. "Hopi Flag." *The Hopi Tribe Official Website*, 2020. www. hopi-nsn.gov/tribal-services/hopi-veterans-services/ hopi-flag/.

10. "History of Hopi Kachina Dolls." *History of Dolls*, 2020. www.historyofdolls.com/doll-history/history-of-hopi-kachina-dolls/.
11. *Www.pinterest.com*. i.pinimg.com/736x/58/0f/6e/580f6e6b1ed02ce1312e88b036f36dcf--puerto-rico-roots.jpg.
12. allthatsinteresting.com/wordpress/wp-content/uploads/2018/08/what-caused-the-decline-of-mayan-civilization.jpg.
13. *Ignboards.com*. www.latinamericanstudies.org/columbus/columbus-voyages.jpg.
14. https://assets.atlasobscura.com/media/W1siZiIsInVwbG9hZHMvcGxhY2VfaW1hZ2VzL2QzYjM0MGUyLTU0NzQtNDI3ZS05NzZiLTYxODUxZjY3MjMxZTJkOGFkYTViNTlhODEyZDgwZV9jaG9jdGF3X2lyaXNooX25ldy5qcGciXSxbInAiLCJ0aHVtYiIsIngzOTA-Il0sWyJwIiwiY29udmVydCIsIi1xdWFsaXR5IDgxIC1hdXRvLW9yaWVudCJdXQ/choctaw_irish_new.jpg
15. https://www.tripadvisor.co.uk/Tourism-g211876-Midleton_County_Cork-Vacations.html.
16. www.americanindianmagazine.org/story/naal-tsoos-sani. Accessed February 22, 2021.

BIBLIOGRAPHY BY CHAPTER

Prologue

Collaborators, Guest. "Mental Health Statistics in Native Americans: Numbers Don't Lie." *Discovery Mood And Anxiety Program*, September 26, 2019. discoverymood.com/blog/mental-health-statistics-in-native-americans-numbers-dont-lie/.

"The Fourth Voyage and Final Years." *Encyclopedia Britannica*. Encyclopedia Britannica, Inc., 2020. www.britannica.com/biography/Christopher-Columbus/The-fourth-voyage-and-final-years.

Wikipedia. "Spanish Conquest of Honduras." *Wikipedia*. Wikimedia Foundation, September 24, 2020. en.wikipedia.org/wiki/Spanish_conquest_of_Honduras.

The Hopi People

Benson, Brittany. "Taxable Tribal Payment Misconceptions." *The Tax Institute at H&R Block*, August 18, 2020. www.thetaxinstitute.com/insights/individual-taxation/misconceptions-abound-in-the-realm-of-native-american-tribal-income-taxation/.

Encyclopedia Britannica, Editors of. "Hopi." *Encyclopedia Britannica*. Encyclopedia Britannica, Inc., 2019. www.britannica.com/topic/Hopi.

Gannon is a journalist based in Berlin, Megan I. "The Knotty Question of When Humans Made the Americas Home."

SAPIENS. Joanne McSporran/PLOS ONE, September 4, 2019. www.sapiens.org/archaeology/native-american-migration/.

"Hopi." *Wikipedia.* Wikimedia Foundation, November 19, 2020. en.wikipedia.org/wiki/Hopi.

Mann, Charles C. *1491 New Revelations of the Americas before Columbus.* Vol. 1. Vintage Books, 2011.

McLeod, Toby. "Hopi Prophecy-A Timeless Warning." *Sacred Land,* April 4, 2020. sacredland.org/hopi-prophecy/.

"Navajo Hopi Land Dispute." *Hanksville.net,* March 20, 1997. hanksville.net/maps/az/navhopi.html.

Padgett, Ken. "Guide to Hopi Kachina (Katsina) Dolls." *Guide to Hopi Kachina Dolls,* 2005, kachina.us/.

Parry, Wynne. "Tribal Fates: Why the Navajo Have Succeeded." *LiveScience.* Purch, November 17, 2011. www.livescience.com/17086-navajo-tribal-fate-jared-diamond.html.

"Poverty Among the Hopi." *NPR.* NPR, October 17, 1998. www.npr.org/templates/story/story.php?storyId=1000821.

"Pueblo Indians." *Encyclopedia Britannica.* Encyclopedia Britannica, Inc., May 15, 2020. www.britannica.com/topic/Pueblo-Indians.

says: Deanna Johnston Clark, et al. "Native America Homes and Lifestyles." *Legends of America,* 2020. www.legendsofamerica.com/na-hopi/.

Staff, HistoryNet. "Texas Longhorns: A Short History." *HistoryNet.* HistoryNet, August 8, 2016. www.historynet.com/texas-longhorns-a-short-history.htm.

"The Impact of the Navajo-Hopi Land Settlement Act of 1974." *News Report Resolutions,* July 2012. www.nnhrc.navajo-nsn.gov/docs/NewsRptResolution/070612_The_Impact_of_the_Navajo-Hopi_Land_Settlement_Act_of_1974.pdf.

Vernon, Katie. "The Hopi Native American Tribe Is Called 'the Oldest of People.'" *The Vintage News,* February 22, 2019. www.thevintagenews.com/2019/01/11/hopi/.

The Navajo People

"Bosque Redondo: The Navajo Treaties." *Smithsonian National Museum of the American Indian*. Smithsonian Institution, 2019. americanindian.si.edu/nk360/navajo/bosque-redondo/bosque-redondo.cshtml.

Brown, Shayne, director. *No One Is Going to Do It for You. NavajoTraditionalTeachings.com*. YouTube.com, September 28, 2020. www.youtube.com/watch?v=NAOn1J1spjQ.

Brown, Shayne, director. *Sacred Native American (Dine) Landmarks. Navajo Traditional Teachings*. YouTube.com, August 17, 2020. www.youtube.com/watch?v=vBradAQqt6I.

Brown, Shayne, director. *Traditional Native American (Dine) Teachings on Positive Thinking. Navajotraditionalteachings. com*. YouTube.com, August 10, 2020. www.youtube.com/watch?v=dsrQNJ9IsSA.

Brown, Shayne, director. *Wally Teaches about Where the Name Navajo Comes From. YouTube.com*, September 19, 2019. www.youtube.com/watch?v=hddm8KLeZqc.

"Diné." *Navajo Language (Diné Bizaad)*, January 2, 2015. navajowotd.com/word/dineh/.

"Fact Sheet." *Discover Navajo*. Navajo Tourism Department, 2020. www.discovernavajo.com/fact-sheet.aspx.

McNitt, Frank. *Navajo Wars: Military Campaigns, Slave Raids, and Reprisals*. Tucson, Arizona: University of New Mexico Press, 1972.

"Navajo Long Walk to the Bosque Redondo—Legends of America." Legendsofamerica.com. www.legendsofamerica.com/na-navajolongwalk/.

"Navajo Treaty of 1868 < 1851-1875 < Documents < American History from Revolution to Reconstruction and Beyond." Www.let.rug.nl. Accessed February 22, 2021. www.let.rug.nl/usa/documents/1851-1875/navajo-treaty-of-1868.php.

Scott, Author: Caylee. "'If You Don't Have Running Water, How Can You Wash Your Hands?': Lack of Running Water Complicates Coronavirus Suppression on Navajo Nation."

Kcentv.com, April 9, 2020. www.kcentv.com/article/news/ health/coronavirus/if-you-dont-have-running-water-how-can-you-wash-your-hands-lack-of-running-water-in-homes-complicates-coronavirus-suppression-on-navajo-nation/75- -0cc99ab4-60bc-479c-a6cf-09d37a0051ac.

"The Long Walk of the Navajo: Peoples of Mesa Verde." *The Long Walk of the Navajo | Peoples of Mesa Verde.* Crow Canyon Archeological Center, 2014. www.crowcanyon.org/educa-tionproducts/peoples_mesa_verde/historic_long_walk.asp.

Ya-Native. *As I Walk in Beauty*, May 26, 2014. https://yanative. wordpress.com/tag/prayer/.

The Blue Kachina

Arizona State Museum, director. *The Resiliency of Hopi Agriculture:2000 Years of Planting. Https://Statemuseum. arizona.edu/*, April 10, 2018, www.youtube.com/ watch?v=28gAFESNGMU&app=desktop.

Encyclopedia Britannica, Editors of. "Hopi." *Encyclopedia Britannica*. Encyclopedia Britannica, Inc., 2019. www.bri-tannica.com/topic/Hopi.

"Types of Corn." *Native*, June 12, 2018. www.nativeseeds.org/ blogs/blog-news/types-of-corn.

The Hopi and the Virus

"Poverty Among the Hopi." *NPR.* NPR, October 17, 1998, www. npr.org/templates/story/story.php?storyId=1000821.

The Navajo and the Pandemic Part 2

Hussar, W. J., and T. M. Bailey. Projections of Education Statistics to 2021 (NCES 2012-044). National Center for Education Statistics, Institute of Education Sciences, US Department of Education. Washington, DC: US Government Printing Office, 2012.

US Department of Education, Institute of Education Sciences, National Center for Education Statistics. The Nation's Report Card: Civics 2010 (NCES 2011-466). Washington, DC: Author, 2011.

The Navajo and the Pandemic Part 3

Brent, Harry. *Meet the Native American tribe who selflessly sent money to Ireland during the Great Famine.* The Irish Post, August 30, 2019. https://www.irishpost.com/life-style/meet-native-american-tribe-selflessly-sent-money-ireland-great-famine-170734

O'Loughlin, Ed, and Mihir Zaveri. *Irish Return an Old Favor Helping Native Americans Battling the Virus. New York Times*, May 5, 2020. https://www.nytimes.com/2020/05/05/world/coronavirus-ireland-native-american-tribes.html

June 19

Nieman, Donald G. *From Slavery to Sharecropping: White Land and Black Labor in the Rural South, 1865-1900.* Garland, 1994.

"What Was Jim Crow." *What Was Jim Crow–Jim Crow Museum–Ferris State University*, 2020. www.ferris.edu/jimcrow/what.htm.

FURTHER READING

US Native American Relations

1. *1491: New Revelations of the Americas before Columbus* by Charles C. Mann
2. *1493: From Columbus's Voyage to Globalization* by Charles C. Mann
3. *Bury my Heart at Wounded Knee: An Indian History of the American West* by Dee Brown
4. *Indian Givers: How the Indians of the Americas Transformed the World* by Bartolome De Las Casas
5. *A Short Account of the Destruction of the Indies*
6. *An Indigenous Peoples' History of the United States* by Roxanne Dunbar-Oritz
7. *Navajo: A Portrait of a Nation* by Joel Grimes
8. *Dinéjí Na`nitin: Navajo Traditional Teachings and History* by Robert S. McPherson
9. *A Dinè History of the Navajo Land* by Klara Kelly and Harris Francis
10. *Ancient Blood: A Navajo Nation Mystery* by R. Allen Campbell
11. *Book of the Hopi* by Frank Waters
12. *The Hopi Survival Kit: Prophecies, Instructions and Warnings Received by the Last Elders* by Thomas E. Malis
13. *Footprints of the Hopi People: Hopihiniwtiput Kuveni'at* by Leigh Kuwanwisima, T. J. Ferguson, and Chip Colwell.

14. *The Fourth World of the Hopis: The Epic Story of the Hopi Indians as Preserved in Their Legends and Traditions* by Harold Courlander
15. *American Holocaust: The Conquest of the New World* by David E. Stannard.
16. *Blood and Thunder: An Epic of the American West* by Hampton Sides.

Conquest and Colonization Outside the American Continents

1. Miriga, Judy. *The Challenge of Decolonization in Africa*, Socio Economic Network, May 24, 2015. socio-economicforum50.blogspot.com/2015/05/the-challenge-of-decolonization-in.html.
2. Rana, Junaid. "The Challenge of Decolonization." *The Islamic Monthly*, November 17, 2016. www.theislamic-monthly.com/the-challenge-of-decolonization/.
3. Ghazoul, Ferial J. *Edward Said and Critical Decolonization*. American University in Cairo Press, 2007.
4. Said, Edward W. *Culture and Imperialism*. Vintage Books USA, 1994.

Informative and Interesting Fiction

1. *Heart Berries* by Therese Marie Mailhot
2. *The Grass Dancer* by Susan Power
3. *An American Sunrise: Poems* by Joy Harjo
4. *Cogewa the Half Blood* by Mourning Dove
5. *Her Land Her Love* by Evangeline Parsons Yazzie
6. *Navajos Wear Nikes: A Reservation Life* by Jim Kristofic
7. *Trail of Lightning* by Rebecca Roanhorse

African American History in the US

1. Little, Becky. "The Last Slave Ship Survivor Gave an Interview in the 1930s. It Just Surfaced." *History.com.* A&E Television Networks, May 3, 2018. www.history.com/news/zora-neale-hurston-barracoon-slave-clotilda-survivor?li_source=LI.
2. Little, Becky. "Descendants of Last Slave Ship Still Live in Alabama Community." *History.com.* A&E Television Networks, May 21, 2018. www.history.com/news/slaves-clotilda-ship-built-africatown.
3. "What Was Jim Crow." *What Was Jim Crow–Jim Crow Museum–Ferris State University*, 2020. www.ferris.edu/jimcrow/what.htm.
4. Public Broadcasting Services. "Sharecropping." *PBS.* Public Broadcasting Service, 2017. www.pbs.org/tpt/slavery-by-another-name/themes/sharecropping/.
5. Nieman, Donald G. *From Slavery to Sharecropping: White Land and Black Labor in the Rural South, 1865-1900.* Garland, 1994.
6. Nieman, Donald G. *African American Life in the Post-Emancipation South: 1861-1900: a Twelve Volume Anthology of Scholarly Articles.* Garland Publishing, 1994.
7. Nieman, Donald G. *Church and Community among Black Southerners, 1865-1900.* Garland Publishing, 1994.
8. Nieman, Donald G. *African Americans and Southern Politics from Redemption to Disfranchisement.* Garland Publishing, 1994.
9. Nieman, Donald G. *African Americans and the Emergence of Segregation 1865-1900.* Garland Publishing, 1994.
10. Nieman, Donald G. *Black Freedom, White Violence: 1865-1900.* Garland Publ., 1994.
11. Nieman, Donald G. *The Politics of Freedom: African Americans and the Political Process during Reconstruction.* Garland Publishing, 1994.

12. Nieman, Donald G. *The Freedmen's Bureau and Black Freedom*. Garland Publishing, 1994.
13. Gibbons, Akil, director. *Genealogist Who Tracks Down Modern-Day Slavery*. *YouTube*. VICE News, 2018. www.youtube.com/watch?v=6OXbJHsKB3I.

RESOURCES

1. The Navajo Hopi COVID-19 Relief Fund (https://www.gofundme.com/f/NHFC19Relief)
2. The Pueblo Relief Fund (https://pueblorelieffund.org/home)
3. First Nations Development Institute (https://www.first-nations.org/)
4. The Hopi Foundation (https://www.hopifoundation.org/)
5. The Navajo Water Project (https://www.navajowater-project.org/)
6. Kinlani/Flagstaff Mutual Aid
7. (https://kinlanimutualaid.org/?fbclid=IwAR2ol-lE3MXxQ4AmXA4m9db64Zt0kxZcDTSMgK-5M9E4dBJCvSY5m9i2Nj1fQ)
8. NDN Collective (https://ndncollective.org/)
9. Seeding Sovereignty (https://seedingsovereignty.org/)
10. Decolonizing Wealth (https://www.decolonizingwealth.com/)
11. Native American Heritage Association (https://www.naha-inc.org/)
12. (https://www.navajonsn.gov/News%20Releases/NNOOC/2021/210421_BT_NNOOC_Navajo_Population_Increase_FINAL.pdf)

ABOUT THE COVER DESIGNER

Travis Tubinaghtewa is from the village of Sitsomovi on the First Mesa of the Hopi Nation. Tubinaghtewa is of the Deer Clan and paints to express himself and connect with his culture. Sometimes he also creates traditional Hopi carvings. In his words, "Art has been my passion my whole life, but the past few years, I've been really dedicating my life to it." To connect with Travis, reach out to him on LinkedIn as travisTubinaghtewa or Instagram @trav_the_artist

ABOUT THE AUTHOR

J. A. M. Kinsella, an atypical citizen, lived in a tyrannical Regime disguised as a democracy. As was the case with most Regime citizens, Kinsella was oblivious to the country's secrets. That all changed one day when Kinsella saw two impoverished and down-trodden Native Americans in a grocery store. This brief glimpse into the plight of the First Nations initiated Kinsella's realization that her home country was a quasi-dictatorship. Since this observation, Kinsella desired to help out. A recent pandemic that led devastation of indigenous communities prompted her to act. She wrote this book with the intention of exposing the enduring Native American oppression in the twenty-first century.

Printed in the USA
CPSIA information can be obtained
at www.ICGtesting.com
LVHW042101260824
789301LV00001B/157